# Consider the Stars

## Francis S. Green

**TEACH Services, Inc.**
PUBLISHING
www.TEACHServices.com • (800) 367-1844

World rights reserved. This book or any portion thereof may not be copied or reproduced in any form or manner whatever, except as provided by law, without the written permission of the publisher, except by a reviewer who may quote brief passages in a review.

The author assumes full responsibility for the accuracy of all facts and quotations as cited in this book. The opinions expressed in this book are the author's personal views and interpretations, and do not necessarily reflect those of the publisher.

This book is provided with the understanding that the publisher is not engaged in giving spiritual, legal, medical, or other professional advice. If authoritative advice is needed, the reader should seek the counsel of a competent professional.

Copyright © 2023 Francis S. Green
Copyright © 2023 TEACH Services, Inc.
ISBN-13: 978-1-4796-1557-5 (Paperback)
ISBN-13: 978-1-4796-1558-2 (ePub)
Library of Congress Control Number: 2023900436

Unless otherwise stated, all Bible text references are taken from the King James Version (KJV) of the Bible. Public domain.

Bible texts marked (NKJV) are taken from the New King James Version ®. Copyright © 1982 by Thomas Nelson. Used by permission. All rights reserved.

*Dedication*

*For my longtime friends of the Mead family, including David, Nohemi, Silvana, Mary, Maurice, and Tara.*

# Table of Contents

1. Consider the Stars ................................................... 11
2. Our Jesus ............................................................ 13
3. Sing Unto God ........................................................ 14
4. Beyond Our Love ...................................................... 15
5. Some Things I Know ................................................... 16
6. The First of Love .................................................... 17
7. An Understanding Heart ............................................... 19
8. His Face ............................................................. 21
9. Always and Forever ................................................... 22
10. Your Heart Belongs .................................................. 23
11. Given to God ........................................................ 24
12. The Fear of the Lord ................................................ 26
13. The Gospel of Grace ................................................. 27
14. Twelve Common Men ................................................... 28
15. Cup of Remembrance .................................................. 29
16. The Given Word ...................................................... 30
17. Prayer for the Coming Day ........................................... 32
18. Beneath Thy Wings ................................................... 33
19. His Peace ........................................................... 34
20. The Gift That Fills My Soul ......................................... 35
21. God's Man at Hacksaw Ridge .......................................... 37
22. Taking Stock ........................................................ 38

23. The Offered Hand ................................................ 39
24. Mercy in the Sky ................................................ 40
25. Another "Ellis Island" .......................................... 42
26. The Other Key .................................................. 43
27. Though We Are Unaware ..................................... 45
28. Wordless Remorse ............................................. 46
29. Praying to Your Friend ........................................ 47
30. The Human Soul ............................................... 49
31. The Woman at the Well ....................................... 50
32. Remember ...................................................... 52
33. I Sleep .......................................................... 54
34. The Greater Light .............................................. 56
35. The Prodigal ................................................... 57
36. Don't Wound Your Soul ....................................... 58
37. The Rich Young Ruler ......................................... 60
38. A Place of Joy .................................................. 61
39. A Prayer When Dying ......................................... 62
40. Greater Than All ............................................... 63
41. Almighty Arms ................................................. 64
42. Wife of Thy Youth ............................................. 66
43. Where Are the Nine? .......................................... 67
44. Freedom ........................................................ 69
45. His Leading .................................................... 70
46. Stand ........................................................... 71
47. The Coming of Night .......................................... 73

48. Our Great Reward.................................................. 75
49. Show Us the Father............................................... 76
50. The Gift of God .................................................... 78
51. Look and Live ...................................................... 79
52. Thomas at His Best............................................... 81
53. The Arm That Is Not Shortened ............................ 82
54. Two Tiny Coins ..................................................... 83
55. Blessing My Lord.................................................. 84
56. A Song from Long Ago......................................... 85
57. A Christian's Seven Wonders................................ 87
58. Relics and Reality................................................. 89
59. When Breath Departs ........................................... 90
60. Cry of the Hebrews .............................................. 92
61. The Flame ............................................................ 92
62. So Near to Love ................................................... 94
63. Warmer in the Son................................................ 96
64. Cry Out to Him ..................................................... 98
65. The Children's Bread............................................ 99
66. A Bowl of Stew ................................................... 101
67. Even When He Turns Away ................................ 103
68. Written in the Sand ............................................. 105
69. The Fatal Way..................................................... 107
70. His Mother at the Cross ..................................... 109
71. The Teacher........................................................ 111
72. Call Me ............................................................... 113

73. Naked on the Cross.................................................114
74. Last Word to the World............................................116
75. The Longing of My Heart .........................................117
76. A Jew by Blood ......................................................119
77. To Us There Is the Father ........................................121
78. My Kindred............................................................122
79. A Dying Daughter ...................................................123
80. The God We've Known.............................................125
81. Old Glory...............................................................126
82. His Words unto the Common ...................................128
83. The Earth in Place..................................................130
84. A Nature of Kindness..............................................132
85. Little More than Forty.............................................134
86. The Surgeons and the Book ....................................136
87. Heart Cry ..............................................................138
88. Where Is Thy Trust?................................................139
89. A Time for Peace ...................................................140
90. Consuming Fire......................................................141
91. We Want a King......................................................143
92. Good Master..........................................................145
93. The God Our Hearts Embrace ..................................147
94. Fugitives from Glory................................................148
95. Our Unbelieving Prayers .........................................149
96. Graven Hands—Wounded Hands..............................151
97. He Sees It All.........................................................153

| | | |
|---|---|---|
| 98. | In His Heart | 154 |
| 99. | Son of David | 156 |
| 100. | Some Treasures Can't Be Lost | 158 |
| 101. | Wrong Side of the Door! | 159 |
| 102. | Thy Flag Unfurled | 161 |
| 103. | Yahweh Had a Son | 162 |
| 104. | The Anguished Cry | 163 |
| 105. | The Offer | 164 |
| 106. | A Dream in Galilee | 165 |
| 107. | Waking to the Light | 167 |
| 108. | A Righteousness Received | 169 |
| 109. | The Living Stone | 170 |
| 110. | A Sacrifice That Breaks the Heart | 171 |
| 111. | The God of Slaves | 173 |
| 112. | A Very Special Man | 175 |
| 113. | The Sinner at Simon's House | 177 |
| 114. | The World Before | 178 |
| 115. | The Child Grows | 180 |
| 116. | Facing the Tempter | 182 |
| 117. | Wine and Wisdom | 184 |
| 118. | Lazarus Come Forth! | 186 |
| 119. | The Olive Grove | 188 |
| 120. | Upon This Hill for Dying | 190 |
| 121. | The Rising of the Son | 192 |
| 122. | Traveling to Emmaus | 193 |

123. The Thorn .................................................... 195
124. Before the Throne of Nero ....................................... 197
125. The Trump Shall Sound........................................... 199

# Consider the Stars

If one should look upon the earth,
And view the sins of man,

He just might think, we came from naught;
Devoid of God or plan.

But, look you to the heavens,
That shine in glory still:

How can one gaze upon the stars,
Without a heart that thrills?

The wonders of the sky above,
Puts unbelief to shame!

The beauty of our canopy,
The hand of God proclaims!

The vastness of the heavens,
Exceeds the minds of men!

Yet, even so, the heart can know,
A great and mighty Friend—

Who fashions our reality,
And all the mind can know!

Great Spirit He of everything,
That feeds the human soul!

*"When I consider thy heavens, the work of thy fingers, the moon and stars, which thou hast ordained; What is man, that thou art mindful of him?"*
*Psalm 8:3*

\*\*\*

The following was the inspiration for the first six stanzas of this poem.

*"I never behold the stars that I do not feel that I am looking in the face of God. I can see how it might be possible for a man to look down upon the earth and be an atheist, but I cannot conceive how he could look up into the heavens and say there is no God."*
*Abraham Lincoln*

Quoted in "The Women in Lincoln's Life" p. 81, by H. Donald Winkler, Rutledge Hill Press.

# Our Jesus

Jesus wasn't mean, nor was He spiteful;
Never was He cruel or hard at all!

Thoughts that were unclean or action hateful,
Not found were these, nor any that appall!

Reverently He lived unto His Father
And His kindness was as natural as could be!

Oh! Jesus, will You come forth and abide here,
And let Your holy life be found in me?

Unselfishly You lived and cared for others
And never did You anything for show!

Never were You false or just pretending;
Yours, was a natural goodness of the soul!

You always took the part of those we turn from.
The shamed and every outcast You did know!

Oh Father! Take our hearts of stone from out us,
And give a life like His unto us all!

*"The Father hath not left me alone; for I do always those things that please him."*
*John 8:29*

*"A bruised reed shall he not break, and smoking flax shall he not quench."*
*Matthew 12:20*

# Sing Unto God

Sing unto God in your weakness:
O, praise give the Lord in your fear!

Strength of the heart, comes in faith spoke aloud:
Might grows in words that endure!

Cry forth the truth He has written:
Speak with the beauty of song!

Life, He pours into words that you speak:
Darkness is conquered and gone!

Speak forth the praise of your Father:
Show forth His glorious Son!

Then, chains of the night fall from off you:
And lies of the snake are undone!

"Glory to God in the highest!"
O, call from the depts of your soul!

Then, rise! with songs of the morning:
And live in the glory you know!

*"As for me, I will call upon God; and the Lord shall save me."*
*Psalm 55:16*

# Beyond Our Love

There is a love, beyond our love:
More Sacred!
A love of which, we really, can't conceive!

We reach for it and try, somehow,
To grasp it! Oh, how, it calls
On us, to but believe!

Like newborns, come into light,
From darkness!
When all that we, have understood, is night!

Yet, sense, that there is care, beyond our knowing,
That seeks for us from up
Amongst the heights!

How could such love come down;
And we perceive it?
How could that light be seen,
By we the lost?

That love has found a way,
That it can show us:
Distilled for understanding,
On a cross!

*"He that loveth not knoweth not God; for God is love."*
*1 John 4:8*

# Some Things I Know

I know I am but common dust of Eden,
From which You've granted flesh and blood to be.

I know that there are worlds unseen about us.
But more than this, I know You care for me!

I know that there are multitudes, now sleeping,
Who yet, are kept within the heart of Christ.

And know that they'll arise, when He shall call them.
And that iniquity will not come twice!

I know that there are messengers from heaven,
Who keep us from the dark, by mighty arm.

And if we choose to walk within Thy keeping,
Our flesh may die, yet hearts are kept from harm!

I know this is a world steeped in evil,
And yet, we all may walk in golden light.

For this our earth holds both a curse and blessing,
And we may live in day, or dwell in night!

I know that there are holy arms about us,
Which never of volition let us go.

For there is One who died that we not perish!
And there is one true love that we must know!

*"And this is life eternal, that they might know thee the only true God,
And Jesus Christ, whom thou hast sent."
John 17:3*

## The First of Love

The first of love we ever know,
Is to be learned at home.

Here, God designed that we should see,
And learn love from our own.

But should the ones who brought us life,
Yet fail, love to show,

There is a love beyond our kin,
That anyone can know.

For He who is our light of day,
Will speak to any heart that prays.

And bring us human love as well,
If of our needs to Him we tell.

But place your soul within His hands,
Who knows those needs and for them plans.

Your cries for love He longs to fill.
Our mighty God: He loves us still!

*"When my father and my mother forsake me, then the Lord
will take me up."
Psalm 27:10*

# An Understanding Heart

An understanding heart:
He would not ask for less!
To understand both man and maid,
Was Solomon's request.

He scorned to ask for treasure,
Long life or rank revenge;
But asked of God, for help to rule,
And be his lifelong friend!

The Lord was pleased, His servant,
Had made such pure request:
And only wished as sovereign King,
That he might do his best!

God gave to him true wisdom,
To rule as Heaven's friend;
And added wealth unto him,
And honor among men!

As Solomon, my ask of Thee,
Is as thy kingly friend:
An understanding heart O Lord,
To reach the hearts of men!

I ask the wisdom, come from Thee,
That has its roots above.
That I may lead some questing souls,
Unto Thy throne of love!

O Lord be Thou my wisdom,
And let me walk with Thee!
And let my work and all my words,
Be those You give to me!

*"But unto them which are called … Christ the power of God, and the wisdom of God."*
*1 Corinthians 1:24*

# His Face

His features were not lovely,
Except, perhaps His eyes!

The windows of a wondrous soul,
That cannot be disguised!

His face, it held no beauty,
Except, for His dear smile!

Especially for the little ones,
When He would rest awhile!

A plain, perhaps a homely face
Its treasure hid within!

But oh! The glory we shall see,
When He shall come again!

*"He hath no form nor comeliness; and when we shall see him,
there is no beauty that we should desire him."
Isaiah 53:2*

# Always and Forever

Always and forever!
The love of Christ is true.
If any turns away from love,
It is not Christ, but you!

Always and forever!
He's had a faithful heart,
And does not will the souls He's made,
Should dwell from Him apart.

Always and forever!
His promises shall stand!
And all may put our trust in Him,
Who gave His all for man!

Always and forever!
In Him our hearts shall dwell:
Rejoicing in two wounded hands,
That doeth all things well!

*"He hath done all things well."*
Mark 7:37

# Your Heart Belongs

When sin attacks unwitting flesh,
Yet, cannot touch the soul!

Your heart belongs to one you love,
and whom your heart doth know!

Because your mind belongs to Christ,
And you've been born, not once, but twice!

He's hid the treasure of your life,
Within His endless soul!

When wickedness attacks your mind,
His love is strong at just that time!

And if His strength your life would show,
Just call upon that Endless Soul!

Ignore the inward clamor,
Of lust and all its kin!

And let your mind attune itself,
To precious words from Him!

Partake the grace of Heaven:
The theme of angel song!

Then turn from every voice of sin,
And know your heart belongs!

*"My heart is fixed, O God, my heart is fixed. I will sing and give praise."*
Psalm 57:7

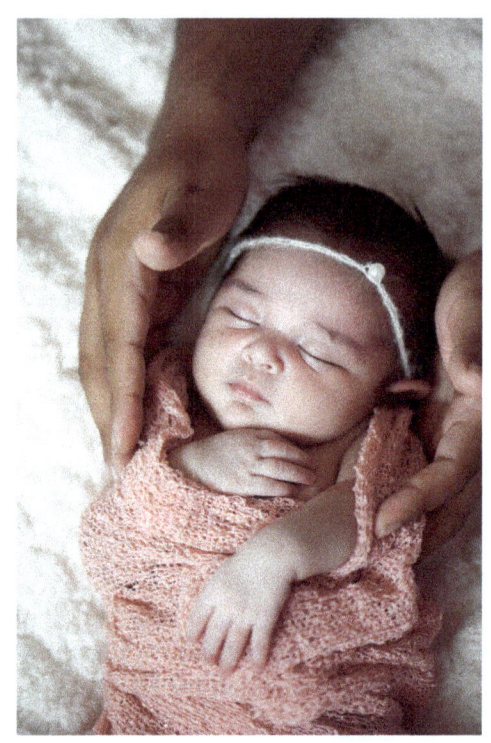

# Given to God

Do take this little child Lord,
Whom in my arms I bring:

And make this tiny treasure Thine;
This infant soul, O King!

This lovely babe, you've given me,
I now give back to you!

Do let its heart and life O Lord,
Be ever good and true!

Oh, grant this child to grow in grace,
And ever sing Thy praise;
And live in faithful love to Thee,
For all its shining days!

*"I will give him unto the Lord all the days of his life."*
*1 Samuel 1:11*

# The Fear of the Lord

The fear of the Lord is a treasure!
A blessing near gone from the earth.

Most have forgotten to reverence the Name,
That gave all creation it's birth!

The heart of the wicked's emboldened,
To scorn at the name that's Divine!

Like those who mocked at the foot of the cross,
"Come down! We'll believe you this time!"

The fear of the Lord, that's held evil in check,
Has nearly been lost from the heart!

Now all the foundations of life on the earth,
Are rotting and falling apart!

The fear of the Lord is a treasure indeed!
That brings forth repentance in man.

Without it, the mockers but speak their own doom,
And none of their stubble shall stand!

*"The fear of the Lord is his treasure."*
*Isaiah 33:6*

# The Gospel of Grace

"The gospel of the grace of God,"
It lights the hearts of men!
No more, cold deities of stone,
But grace from one dear Friend!

Good news indeed! A call to all,
If souls will but believe!
To turn from self. Put trust in Him!
And His free gift receive!

"The Gospel of the grace of God,"
At last! a path that's true!
Herein is found, the way to home,
For every heart renewed!

*"The ministry which I received from the Lord Jesus, to testify to the gospel of the grace of God."*
*Acts 20:24*

# Twelve Common Men

Twelve common men, chose by Him,
To light the world anew!
And carry forth His holy words,
And deeds, to me and you!

Twelve common men to carry light:
Unlikely though they seemed!
Twelve common men, called from the dust,
To work, beyond their dreams!

With faltering steps, they learned from Him,
Of heaven's way and creed!
And finally came to live the truth,
By following His lead!

These common men, unfilled with self,
The same, could love and hear Him!
Unlike the learned, in their conceits,
Who only fought and feared Him!

O Lord! Grant us, young learning hearts,
And wisdom's voice, to hear it;
Avoiding traps of vain conceit:
Complacence, how we fear it!

*"Ye have not chosen me, but I have chosen you, and ordained you, that ye should go and bring forth fruit."*
*John 15:16*

# Cup of Remembrance

Don't forget our wounded Lord in heaven.
Recall to mind, the blood once shed for you!
Break the bread and drain the cup remembering
And let these simple acts your faith renew!

With longing, He would see His brethren gathered,
And dine within the kingdom, there with thee!
One vast believing family there assembled,
And every one, a soul beloved of He!

That day shall come, for Christ Himself declared it!
No fruit of vine will taste He until then.
Full sweet will be the wine, then poured for sharing;
The best He hath reserved until the end!

*"This cup is the new testament in my blood: this do ye, as oft as ye drink it,
in remembrance of me."*
*1 Corinthians 11:25*

*"I will not drink henceforth of this fruit of the vine, until that day when
I drink it new with you in my Father's kingdom."*
*Matthew 26:29*

*"Thou hast kept the good wine until now."*
*John 2:10*

# The Given Word

Shall the given Word stand,
That He gave unto man?
Till the mountains sink into the sea!

Till the sun rise no more,
On all we adore!
Till all that breathe pass away!

All here, waxes old as a garment!
Even stone wears down in its day!

But the Word of the Lord is immortal!
Just as He who hears when we pray!

The Word spoke on high, can't be broken!
Though the heavens themselves pass away!

All He says, it shall stand fast forever!
As the Word of the Ancient of Days!

*"The word of the Lord endureth forever. And this is the word which by the gospel is preached unto you."*
*1 Peter 1:25*

*"Heaven and earth shall pass away, but my words shall not pass away."*
*Matthew 24:35*

# Prayer for the Coming Day

May the coming of
The rising Sun
Lay clear before
The heart,

The privilege
And the miracle,
Of every morning's
Start.

And may we come
To realize,
Allotted days
Are few.

Hence, spend them wise,
In gratitude,
For chances
Yet renewed!

*"My voice shalt thou hear in the morning, O Lord; in the morning will
I direct my prayer unto thee, and will look up."
Psalm 5:3*

# Beneath Thy Wings

Beneath the shelter of Thy wings,
Thy refuge spreading near;

This hiding place, it keeps my soul,
From thoughts of sin and fear!

My strength, it often fails me,
But Thou my God art strong!

And 'neath the shadow of Thy strength,
My heart cries out in song!

Here in this secret place of power,
My heart is close to Thee;

And fog of dark temptations lift;
Once more my soul can see!

Thy feathers are a mighty shield—
A shelter tested true!

And here my troubled heart finds rest,
Beneath these wings of You!

*"He shall cover thee with his feathers, and under
his wings shalt thou trust."
Psalm 91:4*

# His Peace

"Peace on Earth."
But what is peace?

Unto believing souls,
It is the presence of our Christ,
The Lord whom all may know!

A peace far more than silent guns,
A peace the soul can feel.

A peace that comes,
When other hopes,
Lie in a potter's field!

True peace!
"Not as the world gives peace"

Gives He unto His own,
But peace abiding in a heart
That never walks alone.

*"Peace I leave with you, my peace I give unto you: not as the world giveth, Give I unto you. Let not your heart be troubled, neither let it be afraid."*
*John 14:27*

# The Gift That Fills My Soul

Oh Lord, You are my portion!
My cup is filled by Thee!

Your wondrous love it overflows,
The very heart of me!

It's You who are my passion—
The gift that fills my soul.

Without You, I am merely dust
And this my heart does know!

All earth is seeking heaven,
But this You are to me.

You are the treasure of my heart—
The paradise I see!

You light the Book that You have writ;
Your name signs every page!

And You have walked within my soul—
My life at every stage!

You are my songs come in the night;
You are my Psalmist true:

And I would dwell forevermore
Within the arms of You!

*"My flesh and my heart faileth: But God is the strength of my heart, and my portion for ever."*
Psalm 73:26

# God's Man at Hacksaw Ridge

Desmond came into the war—
A place of man-made hell.
And brought with him, his mighty God,
A God he knew quite well.

He came to mend and save some lives,
A medic new was he.
And since he would not touch a gun,
Seemed mad as he could be.

He did not come to maim or kill,
But make some heroes whole.
His only weapon, trust in God,
Within his very soul.

He carried men from Hacksaw Ridge,
And lowered them to ground.
Mid battle haze and deadly fire,
Some seventy-five he found!

And as he sought among the dead,
His God he did implore:
"Please Lord! In mercy, let me find,
Oh Father! Just one more!"

His arm, it was the Lord's that day!
To seek and save the lost.
And strength was freely given him,
Who would not count the cost!

There came the strength of many men,
Into one slender soul:
That mercy and the might of God,
All witnessing might know!

*"Thou shall not be afraid for the terror by night, nor the arrow that flieth by day."*
*Psalm 91:5*

\*\*\*

Written in honor of Private First Class Desmond Doss, winner of the Congressional Medal of Honor, whom the author met many years ago.

# Taking Stock

I know a Lord who loves me.
I cannot tell you why!

I know the man I've often been,
Would make the angels cry!

My lips I can't call sanctified.
My temper's often short!

And if one measured me for wings,
I'm really not that sort!

I've preached in prison,
Preached in jail;

And Him I've preached,
I've often failed!

In short! I am not much to see.
And yet, pure blood was shed for me!

Call me an abject failure,
Quite overwhelmed with dross!

But I have given up on mirrors!
And cling now to His Cross!

*"For if our heart condemns us, God is greater than our heart."*
*1 John 3:20*

# The Offered Hand

A little child, so very small,
doesn't know too much at all.

You interrupt his little plans,
And yet, he takes your offered hand.

That's natural wisdom undisguised;
He trusts the kindness in your eyes!

And this is just my way with You:
My Master, Lord, and Friend!

You held my hand when I was small.
Do hold my hand again!

I'm really not so learned or tall.
I'm really not so wise at all!

I'll gladly take the hand You give.
Because Your love, it does forgive!

My soul's great needs are not disguised.
I know You see them in my eyes!

I give my trust. I know I must.
For only You are wise!

*"My times are in thy hand."*
*Psalm 31:15*

\*\*\*

This poem was written by the author, after intercepting a toddler pushing a baby in a stroller into the street.

# Mercy in the Sky

Perhaps, you may have wondered,
As a member of our race,
Why we've not destroyed ourselves—
Been blown into space!

Not torn apart by atom blast,
Nor meteor on high!
Why have our sins not doomed us all?
And caused our race to die?

Although our hates are legend,
And we kill as best we can!
Our efforts have not brought about,
As yet, the death of man!

There's reason in the realms above!
There's mercy in the skies!
And something more above our heads,
Unseen by human eyes!

An atmosphere of saving grace,
As real as the air!
Surrounds the earth, whereon we live!
And keeps at bay despair!

The earth is yet protected,
By blood that once was shed.
It's price above the sum of worth,
Of every human head!

The price upon Golgotha paid,
Yet keeps us from our doom!
That cup of love once offered up,
Within an upper room!

Although we've earned extinction,
Yet mercy hovers near!
And His pure atmosphere of grace,
It yet surrounds us here!

*"I saw four angels standing on the four corners of the earth, holding the four winds of the earth, that the wind should not blow on the earth, nor on the sea, nor on any tree."*
*Revelation 7:1*

# Another "Ellis Island"

There's yet, an "Ellis" Isle of hope,
Whose gates will never close.
In the harbor of Redemption,
For all believing souls.

No statue stands in welcome there,
But a rainbow spans the sky,
To greet the refuges of Earth,
Who'll come to dwell on high!

The land they'll enter into,
Upon that golden shore,
Will be a place of endless peace,
And love forever more!

Then, every dream, once born of God,
Herein will be fulfilled.
And passing through those gates of hope,
The human heart will thrill!

*"I go to prepare a place for you."*
*John 14:2*

\*\*\*

For millions of immigrants, Ellis Island, in New York harbor, was their gateway of hope and opportunity in America's "Land of the Free." Its gates closed forever in 1952.

# The Other Key

A woman's not an oven!
To simply grow a man.
Nor is she just an afterthought
In Heaven's master plan!

Oh, gracious Lord, give unto we,
A clearer eye that we may see!
That woman is the other key,
To show us of our Deity!

The EL Shadi of Hebrew
"Great warrior is He"!
A mighty one, the mightiest!
Of warriors there be!

But in that ancient title,
We find this hidden Key!
Our Elohim is also like,
A nursing mother be!

As said the Lord, "I'd gather thee,
As hens gather their young."
Our Deity's reflected true
In daughters as in sons!

Our EL is not a woman!
Nor claims to be a man!
But both are half reflections
Of our Holy Great I Am!

And if we seek the perfect image
Of our own true Deity,
That image is most clearly seen
By joining he and she!

*"There is neither male nor female: for ye are all one in Christ Jesus."*
*Galatians 3:28*

# Though We Are Unaware

Unseen, there is another kind,
Existing in our space:
Great beings that walk this world we know,
And occupy this place!

Some, serving Higher Power
And some of deep decay!
Silent and unseen by us,
Yet, real as the day!

Some, seek the good of humankind,
While others seek our hurt!
Some come to bless from cradle days;
Some hate us from our birth!

Some serve the God who made us all,
And some the beast that be!
And which we do respond to,
That choice is given we!

Some come to bring us suffering,
More than our hearts can bare!
While others come to bless our lives,
Though we are unaware!

*"Be not forgetful to entertain strangers: for thereby some
have entertained angels unawares."
Hebrews 13:2*

# Wordless Remorse

Passing away,
Is another wasted day:
A faded chance,
That one cannot recall.

The morn was bright with promise
But I the stubborn one;
I let the hours slip away,
Until the night had come.

Today, I could have said
that I was sorry.
Or might have found
a gentle thing to do.

So many ways to say,
"Please don't be angry."
But I didn't.
And another day is through.

Don't let the hands of time
Slip by in silence,
While quiet speech can mend
The wound you've made.

Too many hold the words
That tell their sorrow
And send a love worth keeping
To the grave.

*"Be ye angry, and sin not: let not the sun go down upon your wrath."*
*Ephesians 4:26*

# Praying to Your Friend

First prayer I ever prayed! (That wasn't written!)
Except when desperation, spoke from fear!
My very first of praise unto my Maker!
I cherish still His answer, warm and dear.

I did not speak aloud the thoughts of others.
I told no beads, no sacred language sought.
Nor formula from childhood remembered,
But spoke aloud the very words I thought.

My view was from a hill and looking downward,
Upon the roads my youth still longed to know!
The sun in beams descending from the heavens,
Somehow, the scene just filled my empty soul!

"Oh Lord! I love this world You've created!"
For once, I really spoke as to a friend!
'Twas then a holy warmth reached out and touched me!
And never have I felt that warmth again!

As if He spoke, but not a word was spoken!
Embraced, without some loving arms about!
Yet, filling me with joy beyond expressing!
The answer was from Him! I had no doubt!

I've spent long years, just trying to describe it!
There are no words! But this for sure I knew!
That I had met Someone who loved and touched me,
In just a way I can't explain to you!

I know today, it was a loving answer!
A moment rare! To just attract my soul.
There were three hills and I stood on the smallest.
Next day I climbed them all and sought Him so!

From this I learned that prayer is nothing formal,
Nor special words His holy will to bend!
True prayer, it is to bare your heart before Him,
And simply speak unto your dearest Friend!

*"Call unto me and I will answer thee."*
*Jeremiah 33:3*

# The Human Soul

Now, I have given seed of man,
To her my heart did know;
But we did not bring forth a breath,
Nor make a human soul!

The light that lives behind the eyes,
Is more than flesh conceives!
And only comes forth from the God
In whom our hearts believe!

Both, time and life are mysteries,
As is the human soul:
That only answer to the God,
Who fashions all we know!

*"Behold, all souls are mine; as the soul of the father,
so also the soul of the son is mine."
Ezekiel 18:4*

# The Woman at the Well

A woman living long in sin,
For water, comes at noon.
She knows the maids come earlier,
For her would find no room.

Her vessel's carried empty;
Her weary heart as well.
With needs far more than water,
She comes to Jacob's well.

The Master rests beside it,
From the scorching heat of day,
And ask of her a simple drink,
Before she goes her way.

"How ask you of Samaria,
A kindness? You, a Jew!
For as you know, such here as we,
Have naught to do with you."

"You come for water here to draw,
But needs, must come again.
Five husbands in your emptiness,
And not a single friend!"

"My water it doth satisfy:
A well to spring within!
No longer will you draw in vain,
Nor thirst for love again!"

Now you who read, to this take heed!
That water's offered thee!
He calls as well to you today,
"Oh come ye unto Me!"

"Come drink, and quench your burning thirst!
And end your weary quest.
And find a fountain filled with love!
And sweet eternal rest,"

*"Ho, every one that thirsteth, come ye to the waters."*
*Isaiah 55:1*

# Remember

Beaten and tortured
And nailed to a cross!
Still more! There's gathered "holy" men,
To mock salvation's cost!

Drowning in men's hatred,
While bearing all their sin,
Before their eyes, in heaven's light,
One more lost soul, He wins!

A voice calls out beside Him,
"Oh, do remember me!
Please Lord! When You are home again,
Do, please, remember me!"

That cry was for the ages,
As stark as it could be!
And surely, that poor wretch's words,
Are spoken, so, by me!

When better hearts and purer souls,
Are gathered up by Thee,
While calling up the saved of Earth,
Oh, do remember me!

What dark down here befalls me,
But testifies my sin!
But oh, my Lord, I do believe;
And know thou art my friend!

Let blood beyond the earning,
Be yet, applied to me!
I do believe, most holy Lord;
Please do remember me!


*"And he said unto Jesus, Lord, remember me
when thou comest into thy kingdom."
Luke 23:42*

# I Sleep

I cannot hear the prayers you pray.
Your tears I cannot see.
But knew there would be sorrow deep,
In you who cared for me!

I cannot hold you in my arms,
But this I give to you.
I rest not in some urn or grave,
Nor in some mansion true.

I sleep indeed! Till trumpet call!
And Jesus face I see!
Until that day I find repose,
Within the heart of He.

The breath was His, and has returned:
The spark gone back to whence it burned.
My soul in Him is safely kept.
I sleep within His holy depths.

In Him we live and move and breathe,
And find in Him our every need.
In Him, because we have believed,
We never truly die!

But safely sleep within His heart,
In peace, as now do I!
Rejoice my soul is kept in He,
Who died that I might ever be!

I tell you true, He is your Friend!
Believe on Him, whom God did send!
All ye who mourn, my words attend,
And we shall meet again!


*"For in him we live, and move, and have our being."*
*Acts 17: 28*

*"Whosoever liveth and believeth in me shall never die. Believest thou this?"*
*John 11:26*

# The Greater Light

The lesser light it rules the night—
The greater light, the day.

But grace and truth, they came by Christ;
That's how we find our way!

There never was another,
With such great truths to say!

And never were, more blessed words,
For us to hear today!

He taught a God called "Father"
Whose love has never strayed:

A God we trust our souls to,
When down our heads are laid!

Never spoke a man like He!
His words we quote and pray.

Oh, never shone the Sun above
In brighter, clearer rays!

*"Then came the officers to the chief priests and Pharisees; and they said unto them, Why Have ye not brought him? The officers answered, never man spake like this man."*
*John 7:45–46*

# The Prodigal

The father of the prodigal, stands looking down the road,
Where last he saw his errant son, who left his family's fold;
To seek a life of sin and song, and there to sate his lust;
Among companions loose and lost, in whom he's placed his trust.

All money's gone and so the song, with all his faithless friends:
And living low among the pigs, is how his music ends!
"I've had no food in near a week! I fain would dine on husks!
I will not starve, but turn toward home, before there comes the dusk!"

"None care if I should live or die and fall beside the way.
Unto my father I will go and beg a crumb today.
His love I've trampled in the dust. I'm sure he'll view me with disgust!
But pride is gone! To him I go, to ask a job. I must!"

"Oh Father! I was once your son! Do you recall when I was young?
Oh! Just a morsel! Just a crumb! Oh please! For I was once your son!"
Such pleas and cries, in silence dies, when met by love's unchanging eyes!
Lo! Not a word the son he speaks, before he's held by one who seeks!

A robe is brought, the food he sought and love he thought was dead!
And now he rests in loving arms and finds a home instead!
As he, we come to the great I AM, who draws us by His power,
And saves us by a mighty arm, from him who would devour!

No sheep can find the Shepherd, when they are lost and lone;
Tis only He, who seeks them out and bring the helpless home!
Think not, He turns from those who cry! No soul is turned away:
For it is He who draws in love, all who have gone astray!

*"I will arise and go to my father."*
*Luke 15:18*

# Don't Wound Your Soul

Oh, never nip a bud,
Before its blooming!
And never stop a new
And precious heart!

Reject the school
Of self and hardened ego,
And with the cult of death,
Nar' take your part!

Don't ever judge
a miracle unworthy,
Or throw away a love,
Before its start.

Don't wound your soul,
With blood guilt for the helpless;
Nor for a gift of life
That's torn apart.

Someone held and fed you,
When you couldn't.
It was that someone kept you
From the cold.

And 'twill be good,
To know that you had mercy,
When you, yourself, grow helpless
And grow old.


*"Blessed are the merciful: for they shall obtain mercy."*
*Matthew 5:7*

# The Rich Young Ruler

He could have walked with Jesus!
Who loved him at first sight!
And heaven gained by cherishing
Our Lord who is the Light!

He could have found eternal joy,
In following the Lamb!
Instead, he clung to all the dust,
That is the wealth of man!

He's not the first, nor he the last,
To turn from what is real:
And choose the cursed mirage of things,
A fool can hold and feel!

His, could have been, the Hope of earth;
And yet he turned away!
A tragedy repeated still,
In this sad world today!

*"Jesus beholding him loved him."*
*Mark 10:21*

# A Place of Joy

A place of joy! A time for peace!
There endless love we find!
When we immerse in His great words,
That surely were divine!

On dusty roads with Jesus,
Instructed as we go!
His teachings fill the hungry heart
And fortify the soul!

Sermons by the water,
Wonders on the sea,
Dining on His miracles,
Upon the mount with He!

Have Him reach into your heart,
To make your life anew!
Blessing your unworthy self,
As only He can do!

With words none else had uttered,
He fills our questing minds,
And teaches His dear precious truths,
To bless for all of time!

*"The words I speak unto you, they are spirit, and they are life."*
*John 6:63*

# A Prayer When Dying

Stay with me this night O Lord,
And hold me as Thine own.
I would not face the end of life
And coming dark alone.

Do guide me to Thy dwelling place;
This breath returns to Thee.
And may I sleep within Thy heart,
Till Thou shall call for me.

Oh, let me see, when I awake
Great gates flung open wide;
When, at Thy call, I come to Thee,
To ever more abide.

This room is dark, the night is long,
And death, dear friends must part.
Oh, let me rest in Thy sweet love,
In chambers of Thy heart!

*"Thou shalt call and I will answer Thee: Thou wilt have a desire to the works of Thy hands."*
*Job 14:15*

# Greater Than All

"My Father is greater than all," said the Christ,
"And no one can open His hand!"
It's He, that I speak for: For I am the Son,
Of One far greater than man!

He's more than His angels, who fill up the sky,
Yea! More than heaven's great sum!
Before all worlds, He called me His own!
Before the stars were begun!

He charged me to fashion both worlds and men,
For, "My Father is greater than I."
I am the Lamb once slain for sin,
Whom they brought to Jehovah on High!

"My Father is greater than all," says the Lord,
Yea! "My Father is greater than I."
Though Our purpose is one, I serve; I'm the Son,
Of the Ancient of Days in the sky!

*"I go to my Father: For my Father is greater than I."*
*John 14:28*

*"My Father, which gave them me, is greater than all."*
*John 10:29*

## Almighty Arms

Little ones all gathered up,
Within the raging storm;
Cling tightly to dear loving ones,
Who keep them safe and warm!

Strong arms will hold them 'gainst
The dark they cannot understand,
And carry them to find the light
And stand on firmer land.

Dear mothers and determined dads,
They so depend on you!
To bear them to a resting place.
Their hopes reside in you!

But you, who always hold them tight,
You also, know the dark of night!
And so, the plea within your soul:
"I need, as well, strong arms to know!"

Great arms there are!
You cannot see.
And these, unseen,
Surrounding thee!

For there are angels close about,
And One who has atoned!
Reach out and feel those arms about,
Those arms that faith has known.

For these will keep
Your young and thee
Come now!
Believers be!

The night is black
And strong the storm.
And many hearts are lost and torn!
But safe are they from every harm,
Who know and trust Almighty arms!

Ah! live or die! You know it's true!
No real harm can come to you!

*"The eternal God is thy refuge, and underneath
are the everlasting arms."
Deuteronomy 33:27*

# Wife of Thy Youth

Rejoice with the wife of thy youth,
And know that her love is thy truth.
What love has united, let it never be blighted!
Let it blossom like Boaz and Ruth!

Be ravished with the love of thy wife.
She hath given good years of her life.
She bore you your young, your daughters and sons!
Your betrayal would cut like a knife!

Why would you give love to a stranger?
Know you not that your soul you endanger?
He troubles his house, who betrayeth his spouse!
And turns to the arms of a stranger.

Like an ox that hastens to slaughter,
He shames both his sons and his daughters.
Who chooses that day, his own to betray,
Finds another because he hath sought her.

The wife of thy covenant and bride of the youth!
How from her canst thou turn aside?
And treacherously deal with the woman of thy life,
And the vows thou once swore to thy bride?

*"Let none deal treacherously against the wife of his youth."*
*Malachi 4:15*

*"Rejoice with the wife of thy youth. ... and be thou ravished always with her love."*
*Proverbs 5:18–19*

# Where Are the Nine?

On the outskirts of a village,
came Jesus and His men:
When, from afar, ten lepers cried,
His mercy to befriend!

"Oh Lord do look upon us!
We plead thy healing hand!
Have mercy and compassion Lord,
on this poor wretched band!"

"A living death we dwell in
and beg Thy sweet release!
For only You can make flesh new
and bid this curse to cease!"

"Go show thy selves unto the priests!"
Came back the Lord's command,
And quickly did they hasten off,
That desperate leper band!

But one, when he beheld new flesh,
Turned back with shouts of praise,
And fell before his Healer's feet,
In thanks, from where he lay!

"Were there not ten?" said Jesus,
"And now, where are the nine?
For only this Samaritan,
before Me do I find."

"Arise," He said, "and go thy way.
Thy faith hath made thee whole!"
But only one gave praise of heart,
With thankfulness of soul.

Oh Lord do give us grateful hearts.
We seek; oh, let us find!
And God forbid that any here,
Be found among the nine!

*"Were not ten cleansed? But where are the nine?"*
*Luke 17:17*

# Freedom

Freedom is a wondrous thing
(Depending how you use it!)

Free to seek the face of God,
Find love, or turn and lose it!

Free to open wide your heart,
Find light to hold and cherish!

Or free to ruin yourself within,
Seek death and finally perish!

Free to hear the call of life
And turn your ear to harken;

Or free to stop that voice within
And watch the world darken!

Free to find at last a home,
Your purpose and your King!

Free to know forever more,
The God of everything!

*"Where the spirit of the Lord is, there is liberty."*
*2 Corinthians 3:17*

# His Leading

First, just as little children,
He taught us simple rules,
The ABCs of life down here,
With tablets for our school.

We learned beginning rules of health,
And how one ought to eat,
How to use the "rest room,"
And sicknesses defeat!

With, "This is right" and "That is wrong,"
To memorize like children's songs.
He wrote His lessons on our hearts,
Until of soul they were a part!

But then, He taught us of Himself,
By sending His dear Son!
We learned to study Father's heart;
Our middle school begun!

Beyond the rules and ABCs,
We learned what He intends:
That we shall be His very own,
Far more than merely friends!

To walk with Him, as vision grows,
And learn what we shall be!
Eternity to hear His words
And dwell in love with He!

*"Then shall we know, if we follow on to know the Lord:
his going forth is prepared as the morning."
Hosea 6:3*

# Stand

Three hundred Spartans held a pass
Against the Persian horde:
Shoulder to shoulder, shield to shield,
With courage and a sword!

'Twas then the vow passed soul to soul,
Among that mighty band:
"The line shall not be broken where I stand!"

God grant to us as firm a stance,
With Christian for our name!
Deliver from the sins of flesh,
With all their terrible shame!

Vow in defense of Christian homes,
"As soldiers hold their land,
The line shall not be broken where I stand!"

The foe we fight is more than Man!
He seeks more than our blood!
He stole men's hearts outside the ark,
Ere Noah braved the flood!

O Lord bring forth thy fearful sword,
Within Thy mighty hand!
And the line shall not be broken where I stand!

*"For this cause shall a man leave his father and his mother, and cleave to his wife; And they shall be one flesh."*
*Mark 10:7–8*

# The Coming of Night

The wicked rejoice
In the coming of night,
As a cover for violence and sin.

And the devils themselves
Work harder from dusk,
For now, they suspect they can win!

Surely, no one will see
The traps that they lay,
When the shadows are deep in each den.

And the darkness is such,
That the spiritually blind,
May well take death for a friend!

But shining still bright
In blackest of night,
Are angels of light among men!

And these find their way
To the crying of soul,
And to every true prayer they attend!

Now the dark that the wicked
So, trust for their might,
Is just as the noon tide to He!

Who rules over all,
And knows all His own.
And always knows just where they be!

It's not simply coming
Of day, demon's fear!
But He whom to all men is light!

Who saveth His own,
By the power of grace,
And keepeth them all through the night!


*"All things are naked and opened unto the eyes of him with whom we have to do."*
*Hebrews 4:13*

# Our Great Reward

It's not the nations healing leaves,
It's not some mansion fair:
Nor graceful flight to worlds afar,
'Twill make it heaven there!

Nor yet, the flowing stream of life,
Or fruits the tree may bear.
And there's a far, far, greater gift,
Than crowns that we may wear!

Our treasure then, our Great Reward,
Our Lord Himself shall be!
To walk and talk with common flesh,
The likes of you and me!

Surpassing all reunions,
Upon the streets of gold,
'Twill be the blessed fellowship
Of Christ, within our fold.

*"Fear not Abram: I am thy shield, and thy exceeding great reward."*
*Genesis 15:1*

*"Know ye that the Lord he is God: it is he that hath made us,
and not we ourselves; we are his people, and the sheep of his pasture."*
*Psalm 100:3*

# Show Us the Father

I do not say that I will pray,
The Father in your stead.
Who think you gives, both breath and life,
And sends your daily bread?

Your Father makes the sun to shine,
And wills your plants to bud.
And sent His Own to turn your hearts,
Becoming flesh and blood.

You wish to view the Great I Am?
If faith doth live in thee,
Then look upon the Son of Man,
If Father you would see!

The heathen will make them, lies of rock;
Bow down to lifeless stone.
Your Father knows your very heart,
And calls your life His own!

Behold a golden sunrise,
And hold the rich dark earth,
Then drink of good pure water,
As for the truth you search.

For love is writ in every tree,
And fruit you pluck to eat!
His truth is in the stars above,
And lies beneath your feet!

Know, all the idols of the earth,
Are but the devil's sham!
And offer prayer through Christ alone,
To the Ancient, called I Am!


*"He that has seen me hath seen the Father."*
*John 14:9*

# The Gift of God

The gift of God's salvation:
It can be laid aside!
But only by abandoned faith.
The promise still abides!

Fix not your faith in your dark sin,
But in His promise true!
Although your heart condemns you now,
God's greater far than you!

Look not unto your circumstance,
But let God's Word renew!
Confess your deeds, confess your need,
And grace shall come to you!

The difference, great, 'twix Judas,
and Peter, self-condemned;
The latter clung to Mercy's heart,
And faith was born again!

Let God be true, not sinful you:
To Satan charge the lie!
Christ does not turn, from those who yearn,
But heeds the sinner's cry!

*"Look unto me, and be ye saved, all the ends of the earth: for I am God, and there is none else."*
*Isaiah 45:22*

# Look and Live

When Naaman sought a prophet's cure
For loathsome lingering death,
The prophet sent him word to bathe.
Instead, the leaper left!

Surely, more must be required,
Than water and belief!
But only when he bathed in faith,
Did Naaman find relief!

Still, brazen serpents are lifted up!
The word, "But look and live!"
And still, some say, "I don't believe!"
Their faith they will not give!

"Would you be whole?" the Master asked,
A broken, shattered man.
"Rise! Take up thy bed and walk!"
Impossible command!

Yet, when faith received those words,
That helpless man was whole!
The mind may doubt! The mind may carp!
But faith it hears and knows!

So, when He speaks some simple thing,
And says it unto thee,
Be sure, though it seems quite absurd,
By faith, so shall it be!

And how pass we from death to life,
His Kingdom to obtain?
But hear in faith, the Word He speaks
And trust that very same!

*"Jesus saith unto him, Rise take up thy bed and walk."*
*John 5:8*

# Thomas at His Best

"Come, let us go and die with Him,"
Said Thomas, at his best.
When Jesus turned to Bethany,
Then followed on the rest.

And Thomas led the way along,
For all that faithful band.
A noble and a loyal heart,
That's oft forgot by man!

We speak of doubting Thomas,
As though that were his name!
And for that hour of unbelief,
We cover him with shame!

But who can claim a spotless faith,
And cast a piece of stone?
Afraid to let his heart believe,
In fear he stood alone!

Then Thomas saw a miracle:
Touched not His palm or side,
But cried out, "Lord and Deity!"
And knelt at Jesus' side.

So, if you wish to tell his doubt,
Tell love and courage too!
For few would say, as Thomas did,
"I'll go and die with you."

*"Then Thomas, who is called the twin, said to his fellow disciples,
'Let us also go, that we may die with Him.'"
John 11:16, NKJV*

# The Arm That Is Not Shortened

His arm, it is not shortened,
To meet the need of man.
Physician He, for all the ills
We place within His hands.

His power has no limit,
If we will but believe.
In health or ill, we are held close.
He does not turn or leave.

"I never will forsake thee,"
He's promised in His Word.
This is the truth! And we may trust,
In Him, our Mighty Lord!

'Tis He who is our great reward!
We live to do His will.
And when we finally see His face,
Oh, how our hearts will thrill!

All life and breath, is His to give,
Unto the sons of men.
In Him we live, in Him we trust!
Our Lord! And more! Our Friend!

"Behold, the LORD'S arm is not shortened, that it cannot save;
either his ear heavy that it cannot hear."
Isaiah 59:1

# Two Tiny Coins

She only gave two tiny coins,
But gave her heart as well.
And eyes of love beheld it all,
And of her gift did tell.

She gave her necessary food,
Her warmth and shelter too!
And no one else took note at all,
But oh! The Master knew!

Two coins that bless the world yet!
And melt the heart of stone!
Because the Savior blessed the gift,
She gave from love alone.

Like Him, she gave all that she had.
He understood her well!
And of her precious pair of coins,
Still angels love to tell.

The heart that holds back nothing!
But gives all that it hath,
Is very close to Heaven's gates
And walks a holy path!

For Heaven too was once poured out,
And our salvation won,
When Great I Am, gave up for man,
His own beloved Son.

*"She out of her poverty put in all she had her whole livelihood."*
*Mark 12:44, NKJV*

# Blessing My Lord

Bless the Lord, O my soul,
You're all of Heaven that I know!
Healing women, healing men,
My blessed Savior and my friend!

Forgiving all our foolishness,
our frailty and sins!
Redeeming souls, comprised of dust,
And seeking for each one!

Your mercy and Your kindness,
Sweeter to my tongue,
Then any words I've ever known,
Since first my days begun!

To know You is to bless You!
It lifts my heart up higher.
You fill my soul with all good things:
My praising never tires!

O walk with me, till life is gone!
Burn in me like a fire!
In You I know the sum of love,
And meaning of desire!

*"I will bless the Lord at all times: his praise shall continually
be in my mouth."*
*Psalm 34:1*

# A Song from Long Ago

"Bless the Lord O my soul,"
Our David sang, so long ago.
And all there was in him to sing,
He offered to his Mighty King!

Those words comprised a love song!
Not fashioned for a maid.
For David's first love was the Lord!
The same to whom he prayed.

The heart that's joined unto the Lord,
That heart salvation knows!
The ones who give themselves to Him,
They learn true peace of soul.

There's not a contract to be writ,
Of quid and quid pro quo!
But laying down thy life and breath,
Almighty God to know!

Such find the purpose of their life,
And reason for their soul;
When they discover love divine,
And He who loves them so!

Most are content with empty sound,
Some other's prayer to know.
But cries the Mighty Heart above,
"Be hot! Or else, be cold!"


*"I know thy works, that thou art neither cold nor hot:
I would thou wert cold or hot."
Revelation 3:15*

*"Bless the Lord, O my soul: and all that is within me, bless his holy name."
Psalm 103:1*

# A Christian's Seven Wonders

Blessed seven wonders of the earth,
Began with spoken light;
With paradise and life begun,
From out the primal night!

The second wonder of our world,
A man and woman come
From out the wonderous hand of Love,
And humankind begun!

The third great wonder of this world
Beyond all thought or tongue,
That God so loved all humankind,
That He would give His Son!

The fourth of wonders from on high,
With man by sin undone,
That Son stepped forth from heaven's light,
And willingly, did come!

Then came fifth wonder, virgin birth!
And love within a manger!
Yes! Holiness come to the earth,
In one dear tiny stranger!

Sixth wonder of this troubled earth,
Christ nailed to a tree!
To bear the sins of humankind,
And die for you and me!

The seventh wonder of our world?
Ah! Love did rise again!
And in the clouds and light of God,
For us shall come, our Friend!


*"And God saw every thing that he had made,
and behold, it was very good."
Genesis 1:31*

# Relics and Reality

An image on an ancient shroud,
purports to be of Christ.
Devoted flock to gaze on cloth,
Such viewings still entice!

"Now here's the thorns our Master wore!
This spike came from His hand!
And here's a sliver of the cross!
To thrill the heart of man!"

"Mary's milk! And Savior's blood!"
In vials of the same!
There's nothing here that could be true,
Despite such wild claims!

Like blinded men at Calvary,
Who lusted for His robe:
While on the Cross above their heads,
Was heaven's treasure trove!

We are not blessed by "holy stuff,"
That may be put on view!
But by the blood that worketh still,
To save a soul like you!

Men's shrines may hold their relics dear:
They claim beyond all price!
But yet, the whole of heaven's vault,
Cannot contain the Christ!

*"But who is able to build him an house, seeing the heaven and heaven of heavens cannot contain him?"*
*2 Chronicles 2:6*

# When Breath Departs

When goes the light,
And breath departs,
'Tis then, that the entire spark,
Returns to Him, who is eternal fire!

The breath is His—
The life, the flame.
And we do trust that very same,
Who has our faith entire!

We never truly die in Him,
But live within His mind;
Who loves us with an endless love!
With Him our souls we bind.

And when He hath desire for,
The work of His own hand,
He'll call us forth to breathe again,
And in His presence stand!

To live with Him eternally,
Who is our Lord sublime!
And dwell with Him in endless love
Throughout the years of time!

"Then shall the dust return to the earth as it was: and the spirit
shall return unto God who gave it."
Ecclesiastes 12:7

"The hour is coming, and now is, when the dead shall hear the voice
of the Son of God: and they that hear shall live."
John 5:25

# Cry of the Hebrews

Our Father's heart was surly grieved,
By helpless Hebrew pain;
As He would hear repentant prayers,
That rose time and again!

And though they stood in shameful guilt,
He heard their cries of faith.
Then He declared them yet His own,
And saved for His name's sake!

His arm of might not shortened,
Nor yet His gracious hand:
He bore them up and took them back,
Unto Himself again!

As He did then, He does today!
For those, His own who've gone astray!
And every Hebrew, yet He knows,
Who is a Hebrew in their soul!

And not just blood of Abraham
Is heard by He Divine;
No! Any heartfelt prayer of faith,
Can reach Him any time!

*"And the Lord said, I have surely seen the affliction of my people."*
*Exodus 3:7*

# The Flame

Like the burning bush of Sinai,
Your flame is in my heart!
And seems it must consume my life,
My flesh and soul to part!

Yet, like the bush of Sinai,
This self is not consumed!
And not a scent of garments flame,
Within this quiet room!

And while Your flame
Consumes my sin!
New life, new pulse,
Now burns within!

Consuming all
My dross and shame!
I know Thou art
This tongue of flame!

*"And the angel of the Lord appeared unto him in a flame of fire out of the midst of a bush."*
*Exodus 3:2*

# So Near to Love

Three men are dying, nailed up
And naked to the sky!
Two robbers, paying for their crimes—
The third? For you and I!

Christ wore a seamless garment,
Now lying on the ground.
And soldiers note it has a worth;
A thing of value found!

And while the Lord of Glory,
Pays out our price of sin,
They gamble for His under gown
And turn their backs on Him!

The Glory of all human hope
Is just above their heads,
But all they see of value here,
Is what was worn instead!

That One who bled for humankind,
Is still despised by men,
Who'd rather have a bowl of stew
Or thirty coins instead!

While Christ is close enough to touch,
His love held not afar!
How blind the race of sinful men!
What tragic fools we are!

Why would we trade
An endless life, with Him, to live on high?
Why would we die with empty souls?
No hope beyond the skies?

The things we'd rather have than Him,
The things for which we lust—
Will in the end, leave grasping hands,
That hold but worthless dust!

Look up! From empty treasures!
Behold! He dies for thee!
Look up! And see the gift of God,
Those soldiers could not see!

*"Then the soldiers, when they had crucified Jesus, took his garments, and made four parts, to every soldier a part; and also his coat: now the coat was without seam, woven from the top throughout."*
*John 19:23*

\*\*\*

The term "under gown" (in the third stanza) is taken from a suggested rendering found in the amplified Bible, used for the seamless garment (rendered as His "coat" in John 19:23 in the King James Version).

# Warmer in the Son

I walked awhile in warmth of day,
A bright and cheerful one!
Then came the shadow of the trees;
'Twas warmer in the Sun!

Some preach to all, but bitter guilt,
And all mankind undone!
'Tis but an ice-cold offering!
It's warmer in the Son!

Some love to preach a devil's hell,
And torture yet to come!
Their stock in trade, grim, numbing fear.
'Tis better in the Son!

As dry as hills Gilboa,
Which saw no rain or dew!
First, bless the cross, then trust to law.
This path is not for you!

The gospel writ to change the world,
Brings great "good news" to view!
It speaks the mercy of the Lord,
And Christ who died for you!

Men know they are condemned by law:
Sini taught that was true!
But grace and truth came by our Christ—
Salvation's gift for you!

The truth was dimly understood,
Until there came the Christ!
Now ye who found life at the cross,
Will ye chose bondage twice?

Some go the way of works and law;
The Gospel's work undone!
Their path is dark and very cold.
'Tis warmer in the Son!

*"For by grace are ye saved through faith; and that not of yourselves: it is the gift of God: Not of works, lest any man should boast."*
*Ephesians 2:8–9*

# Cry Out to Him

Cry out to Him,
As though your life depended!
Because, this is your
Truly needful state!

Cry out to Him,
Who's mighty to deliver!
For children of your household
And your mate!

Cry out to Him,
To make a way before you!
Deliver from yourself
And sinful dross!

His is the only blood,
By faith, can save you!
For He has borne for all,
Salvation's cost!

*"In my distress I cried unto the Lord and he heard me."*
*Psalm 120:1*

# The Children's Bread

There came a woman of Canaan,
In tears unto the Lord,
And cried to Him for mercy—
Great pleading in her words.

Her daughter had a devil.
A demon vexed her sore.
And grieving for her suffering child,
The mother's heart was tore.

Her pleas were not acknowledged.
He answered not a word.
And then she fell and worshiped low,
Before her mighty Lord.

"I am but sent to Israel."
At last, came His reply.
"How can you ask this thing of me?
How can you justify?"

"For I am sent to Abram's kin,
Their children must be fed.
I cannot give unto the dogs,
Their gift of holy bread."

"The bread's indeed the children's,"
The woman did agree.
"But is there not the crumbs for dogs,
That You can give to me?"

His smile lit the very day!
And drove the mother's fears away.
"O Woman! Great is this thy faith! It shineth from thy soul!

Now go in peace unto thy home;
Thy daughter is made whole."

In soft words and trembling, the plea that she gave,
Comes down to us yet, in the Scripture's own page!
"Though the food is the children's, there falleth the crumbs,
And surely good Master, the dogs getteth some?"

*"O woman, great is thy faith: be it unto thee even as thou wilt."*
*Matthew 15:28*

## A Bowl of Stew

Now, Esau sold his birthright,
Sold heaven for some stew!
For just a moment's hunger,
Away his blessing threw!

For just a bowl of lentils,
For just a bowl of stew!
What is the price to sell your life?
How much to purchase you?

Almost thou doth persuade me—
The truth I nearly view.
But I've no time for you today!
No time for what is true!

For I am such a busy soul,
My hungers I must feed!
Someday I'll stop for heaven's word!
Someday I'll pause to heed!

Upon that day, I'll gladly hear
The truth you bring today,
But I'm too occupied just now,
And must go on my way!

Then came a day of weariness,
And silence in my soul,
And I had naught to occupy—
No special place to go.

Somehow, I knew the night was nigh;
My soul would be required!
And all that heaven offered me,
I never had acquired!

Oh! how I do regret this bowl!
This worthless bowl of stew!
And how I long, my empty heart,
My Lord to fill with You!

*"Lest there be any fornicator, or profane person, as Esau,
Who for one morsel of meat sold his birthright."
Hebrews 12:16*

# Even When He Turns Away

Even when He turns away,
His love is ever true!
And even if the light grows dim,
You'll find Him seeking you!

Yea! Even when, He speaks disgust,
About to spew us out!
Somehow the sound of wooing love,
Is heard from all about!

"How can I give you up?"
He asks, a terrible rending cry!
An inner shout from out His heart,
A mourning from on high!

"Your blood be on your wretched heads!
I leave you to your sins!"
Yet, like His faithful Paul, He leaves,
But dwells close by to win!

A stubborn voice pursues us still!
The Hound of Heaven He!
And Thompson had it right!*
That voice will never let you be!

If we should climb celestial heights,
Or make our beds in Hell,
We cannot flee the voice of love,
That knows us all too well!

And as swift waters wear a rock,
So is His voice to we!
The wood He'll wear upon our doors,
For knocking yet is He!

We'll find it hard to kick the pricks,
As blind are made to see.
Oh soul, fling wide your battered door,
And let salvation be!!

*"I will not execute the fierceness of mine anger ... for I am God, and not man."*
*Hosea 11:9*

\*\*\*

*To read the original poem, "The Hound of Heaven,"
by Francis Thompson, please go to the following link: https://1ref.us/23j
(accessed Nov. 8, 2022).

# Written in the Sand

They seized her in the morning watch, that turns from night to day
And though she tried her best to flee, she could not get away!
Taken in the very act, in torn and flimsy gown;
Paraded past men's hungry eyes and dragged through out the town.

The customer who lay with her and set the trap to spring,
Has quite alluded capture though. (How very strange a thing!)
Now stones are gathered on their way, by hardened "holy" men,
Who claim to serve the Great I Am and purity defend!

They cast their helpless victim then, before the Nazarene,
Who looks upon each darkened heart, within this sordid scene.
A pack of wolves, who seek His blood, the woman's life as well,
And though they claim they're heaven sent; they reek instead of hell!

"Now, Moses says, such should be stoned! Would you her life allow?
Behold! We bring sufficient rocks, to end her even now!"
He kneels down (in deep disgust) and writes upon the ground,
The secrets of their evil lives. (His accuracy astounds!)

"Let he of you who's free from sin, take up the first of stones."
Then each man sees his life laid out, great guilt that each does own.
The deeds they thought were safely hid, have found the light of day!
Now, none can leave quite fast enough, to take themselves away!

The soiled woman in the dust, He raises to her feet.
Oh! Never has she seen a man whose face was half so sweet!
But yet, He knows! And sees within, her life, that's been most vile!
Why does He look forgiving now? Why does He gently smile?

"A new life now is yours to live. Forsake the way of sin.
This day I give you back your breath. A new day to begin!
Your broken cry for mercy, a pardon for you wins.
Your Father says, "Go sin no more" and let Him dwell within!

And you who read, to this take heed. When you would scorn another
And have no mercy but condemn, your sisters and your brothers.
The One above, whose name is Love, knows all your life as well!
He still could write your secrets out, your private bits of hell!

Your sins are writ upon the sand, that He may sweep away!
So, if forgiveness you would seek, remember when you pray:
If you have aught against your kin, or hatred for another;
Be reconciled first to them: your sister or your brother.

*"Neither do I condemn thee: Go and sin no more."*
*John 8:11*

# The Fatal Way

If self you'd recommend by works,
You must forsake the cross.
And count the holy blood of Christ,
It's power to have lost!

Ah! Friend! You've found the fatal way:
To trust in works you do each day!
Yet, every good you'll ever do,
Is but the grace of Christ in you!

You know, you need the Master's blood,
To save your soul, at first!
But in your daily walk of life,
You trust in works and church!

Now, heaven's help you'll give a nod,
And call the Master "friend."
And daily thank the Lord above,
"I'm not as other men!"

So deep in your delusion,
You cannot see the light:
Shining now from Calvary's cross,
To call you from your night!

Somehow, against all Christian sense,
You're sure the good you do,
Will work as well as holy blood,
And Heaven, bring to view!

To gather credit to yourself,
Is wicked soul desire!
With day of judgment drawing nigh,
You're dancing in the fire!


*"O foolish Galatians, who hath bewitched you, that ye should not obey the truth, before whose eyes Jesus Christ hath been evidently set forth, crucified among you? This only would I learn of you, received ye the Spirit by the works of the law, or by the hearing of faith? Are ye so foolish? Having begun in the Spirit, are ye now made perfect by the flesh?"*
*Galatians 3:1–3*

# His Mother at the Cross

Three Marys wept before the cross,
At our dear Master's pain;
But one there was,
Her heart pierced through,
Who bore that suffering same.

Her miracle! The cherished child,
She'd loved since virgin birth;
Her baby small, born in a stall:
The savior of the Earth!

She'd held and nursed the crucified,
Heard his first words, back then;
Once guided his first faltering steps,
A loving mother been!

And now He sees her breaking heart;
His death too much to bear;
And does not let her stand alone,
In pain and dark despair!

"Mother, John is now your son."
He nods at his dear friend.
"She is your mother, now my John,
Oh, tenderly attend!"

With blessing from the Savior's lips,
These two will bond as one;
And Mary has a Savior now
And loving John her son.


*"When Jesus therefore saw His mother, and the disciple whom He loved standing by, He said to His mother, 'Woman, behold your son!' Then He said to the disciple, 'behold your mother!' And from that hour that disciple took her into his own home."*
*John 19:26–27*

## The Teacher

The Law was writ to show my need,
And lead me to His side;
And not a plan to save myself,
For it was He who died!

Only in His presence,
Is freedom won from sin!
Like Peter walking on the waves,
With eyes fast fixed on Him!

A heart of stone, He took from me,
And gave the heart I need.
A still small voice now follows me,
And wondrously it leads!

The Teacher showed my desperate need,
And led me to the cross,
And showed me all my righteousness,
Was emptiness and dross.

And if I say I have no sin,
The righteous words of ten,
Will show my fault and foolishness,
And lead to Christ again!

*"The law was our schoolmaster to bring us unto Christ, that we might be justified by faith. But after that faith is come, we are no longer under a schoolmaster."*
*Galatians 3:24–25*

# Call Me

Call on Me in time of need,
In the union of your soul!
Yours is a voice that I will heed,
My children's voice I know!

Call Me in your gratitude,
In days that shine like gold!
And let Me hear the voice of joy,
When love is in your soul!

I hear you speak, because you trust.
Your cry is dear to Me!
I listen for your prayer at night,
Your quiet time with Me!

I know you listen for My voice,
And would not walk alone!
I'm ever here. You need not fear:
Because you are My own!

*"He hath said, I will never leave thee, nor forsake thee."*
*Hebrews 13:5*

# Naked on the Cross

Our Christ was naked on the cross!
No loin cloth did He wear.
All that the Romans nailed up,
Were nailed, stark and bare!

Intent was not just death and pain,
But that their victim, thus be shamed!
He bore our sins in light of day,
And all pretense was stripped away!

Yes! All the dark we ever did,
Exposed to all, no longer hid!
The fault was ours and all the blame!
And naked He to bear our shame!

Now every pious painter,
Has lent a bit of cloth,
To cover Him and all the shame,
He bore upon the cross.

No doubt, they meant to shelter Him;
Yet, also sheltered sin.
And did not fully show the shame,
Our darkness laid on Him!

Perhaps, if we could fully know,
The pain that tore His heart,
We might give up our darling vice,
And with our evil part!

Ah! Father of Messiah!
And all of us as well!
We know He bore for sinners all,
The very pains of hell!

All things are naked to thine eye,
In darkness as in light.
Oh, let His cross consume our dross!
And cure us of our blight!

*"Jesus…who for the joy that was set before him endured the cross, despising the shame."*
*Hebrews 12:2*

# Last Word to the World

His last word to the world,
Before there comes the end,
Will not be judgment, or the law,
But love of one dear Friend.

To every heart, He will reveal,
Our Maker's deep concern,
For all who will, to die alone,
And choose a day that burns.

"How oft I would have gathered thee,
As mothers do their young."
The saddest words to reach the ear,
Since earth was first begun!

Perhaps, some hearts will open yet:
Cast off their love of sin.
And meet their Lord's own sweet desire,
His love, their souls to win!

Mere fear of flame can move our soul.
To save ourselves be strong!
But only those who fall in love,
With Him, are saved from wrong!

*"As I live, saith the Lord God, I have no pleasure in the death of the wicked; but that the wicked turn from his way and live: turn ye, turn ye from your evil ways; for why will ye die."*
*Ezekiel 33:11*

# The Longing of My Heart

The longing of my heart,
Is just to please You!
And yet, I am both
animal and man.

My flesh cries out!
And it would surely take me,
Away from all the good
Your heart has planned!

Now, all the sins I've known,
They seek to bind me!
And yet, my heart would serve
The great I Am!

Oh! Let me put my trust
In You who love me!
And give no more
Mere promises of sand!

I find, alone,
I never walk on water!
Yet, hand in hand,
So natural it be!

To find the mind of sin
So quickly leave me!
When I am bound to You
And truly free!

Oh! Let my flesh
Be ever more a liar!
And make my life
As You would have it be!


*"O wretched man that I am! Who shall deliver me from this body of death?
I thank God through Jesus Christ our Lord."
Romans 7:24–25*

# A Jew by Blood

I count myself a Jew by blood,
Though, not within my veins!
But Sacred Blood, come down in love,
To make me of the same!

I too am of the chosen race,
That bows before the throne;
Of He who counteth all the stars,
And called the Jews his own!

A Hebrew I, bound for the sky,
Who prays, to Him alone!
Partaker of the Holy Blood
That for all men atoned!

Raw unbelief, brought yours to grief:
Old prophecies fulfilled!
And yet, the heart of He on high,
Is calling to you still!


*"But he is a Jew which is one inwardly; and circumcision is that
of the heart, in the spirit, and not in the letter;
whose praise is not of men, but of God."*
*Romans 2:29*

# To Us There Is the Father

To us there is the Father:
The only God there be!
And only one Yahshua,
Our blessed Lord is He!

All things are of the Father,
And by the Son consist;
For in his first Corinthians,
Paul taught us all of this.

Our Christ declared, in John the fifth
The Father's life within,
As well as judgement of us all,
The Father gave to Him!

"I do not speak my words at all,"
The Master doth declare.
"Nor do the will, I call my own,
But His whose name I bear."

"There is a Father and a Son.
My Father is my holy one.
There is a mountain and a stone.
'Tis He I serve and He alone."

To us there is the Father:
The only God there be!
And only one Yahshua:
Our blessed Lord is He.

*"But to us there is but one God, the Father, Of whom are all things, and we in him; And one Lord Jesus Christ, by whom are all things, and we by him."*
*1 Corinthians 8:6*

# My Kindred

Although there's kin in name and blood,
There's kin of heart to me.
And those who bind our souls most close,
Our own true kindred be!

Ah! Dear beyond all word or thought,
Thy blood once shed for me!
That binds us ever heart to heart.
No closer kin could be!

Thou stands as Father, Mother too!
There are no closer kin than You!
Who makes my life and soul to be:
Thine is the blood most kin to me!

*"There is a friend that sticketh closer than a brother."*
*Proverbs 18:24*

*"For whosoever shall do the will of my Father which is in heaven, the same is my brother, and sister, and mother"*
*Matthew 12:50*

# A Dying Daughter

A ruler of the synagogue, a teacher there of men!
And yet I find, at this terrible time, my own child I can't defend!
My daughter, the joy and light of my life! The dear of her mother and I!
Fades away from our home, soon to leave us alone. We're watching our
sweet child die.

Oh, Yahweh I plead! To your word I pay heed!
But tell me wherein I offend!
I swear to the stars! I'll do better by far! Oh please!
Do not let her life end!
New teacher in town! (A cynic, I frown.) Still, they say,
He can heal and mend!
My fears I can't hide, so I swallow my pride!
For love even pharisees bend!

No doctrines I heed. It's kindness I need!
And power sent down from on high!
Oh, Master please come and save my dear one!
Oh, please, lest my little girl die!
Though I am not his friend, to my pleas He attends,
in kindness receiving my cry.
My pharisee's heart is shamed from the start,
by this Hebrew far better than I!

Often stopped on the way (He turns no plea away!)
His kindness pours forth like a stream!
As we travel to my home, they won't leave him alone!
And then just ahead, there is seen,
A servant of mine, seeking myself to find and his look
nearly makes me despair!
"The teacher trouble no more. Deaths come to our door!
It's too late for a healing back there."

Firm grip on my hand, says this gentle man,
"Fear not but only believe."
At the strength of His voice, with faith as my choice,
fear and dread all drain from my bones!
But then, just ahead, I hear songs for the dead;
paid mourners who sing at my home!
My wife, silent in grief, gets from them no relief;
she might just as well be alone.

"Why do you weep for this dear little sheep?
The child but slumbers in bed."
Mourning turns into jeers, replacing their tears,
"We know when we look on the dead!"
All the mourners put out and turning about
He goes to our child, cold and gray:
Then taking her hand, with a gentle command, says,
"Wake little girl! It is day!"

Then in wondrous surprise, she opens her eyes,
and smiles her sweet face adorn!
Now, death is cast out, and the world turned about,
for here is my daughter reborn!
At last, my wife cries, tears rain from her eyes!
And our Healer says, "She needs to eat."
My wife takes our child, to find her some food.
And I am in tears at His feet!

At our synagogue then, Christ has a firm friend,
once a stern man, becoming quiet mild.
From a cynic with scorn, to a pharisee reborn,
as new a creation as his child!

*"(He) … took her by the hand and called, saying, 'Little girl arise.'"*
*Luke 8:54 (NKJV)*

# The God We've Known

A thousand years unto our God,
Is as a day gone by.
He does not change, with pass of time;
To Him our hearts do cry!

Long years weigh heavy on our frames,
Our days grow dim; yet, He's the same!
Who blessed our hearts when we were young,
And introduced us to His Son!

The same who holds us in repose,
And gives His breath unto our souls!
Oh! bless Him now, when day is done,
The same, as when our hearts were young!

For years of life and joy we've known,
Let thanks ascend unto His throne;
For all the days, His kindness shown,
And love that leaves us not alone!

*"One day is with the Lord as a thousand years,
and a thousand years as one day."
2 Peter 3:8*

# Old Glory

They had so little, but their faith:
(Those pilgrim folk of yore);
Yet sought a land and raised the cross
Upon a pagan shore.

Where fervent worship could be free,
And no man force their prayer.
They left the old world far behind,
To breath of freer air!

Today we are a mighty land,
Where some can live like kings.
Rich is our home, with cities great,
And many shining things!

But faith, perhaps, in short supply,
And worship grown dim.
Now many in our teeming land,
Have quite forgotten Him!

Seems, arms and awesome weaponry
Replace God as our trust.
And all our once great love for Him
Seems fallen into dust!

Now living high, but shorn of faith,
And yet, still blessed with plenty.
It seems the glory once we knew,
Has gone and left us empty!

On this appointed day of thanks,
Praise God our flag still flies!
Oh, may He rest the brave of heart,
Who for this land still die!

How long can any people stand,
Secure without their faith?
God give us back our trust in Thee,
That made our nation great!

*"If my people, who are called by my name, shall humble themselves, and pray, and seek my face, And turn from their wicked ways; then will I hear from heaven, and will forgive their sin, and will heal their land."*
*2 Chronicles 6:36*

# His Words unto the Common

Christ taught the great commandment,
With one to follow on,
And folk they called "the common,"
With Him their hearts did bond!

The common heard Him gladly.
His teachings did astound!
His words to live forever—
So simple! So profound!

It's good to be a common man!
A common woman too!
For you still hear the voice of truth,
When He speaks unto you!

The Mishna and the Talmud
Come readily to mind;
And other comments on the words
That surely are divine.

Why not allow such sacred words
To speak direct to you?
And let the Master teach your mind,
All things profoundly true!

Convoluted, endless arguments,
And words of unbelief!
For these the simple words of Christ,
Will bring the soul relief!

For "never spake a man as He!"
A soldier once declared.
So, open up your heart to Him,
In Bible and in prayer.


*"And the common people heard him gladly."*
*Mark 12:37*

# The Earth in Place

The Master hung this world in space
And knew just what He did.
It must be just so far from Sun,
Or not a thing could live!

The spin He gave, it gave us night,
To rest, as well as day!
He set our orbit fixed and firm,
That it not spin away!

A bit too close and we would burn!
A bit too far, we'd freeze!
Our Maker also made the stars,
At night that all can see!

Our lovely moon gives pale light,
To gladden many a silver night!
And yet, the moon in orbit stays,
That continents not sweep away!

Our ozone keeps most harmful rays
Of radiation from our days.
Though men may come and men may go,
Yet lives this wondrous world we know!

No meteors destroy the earth!
For He decrees it so!
Our orbit is so firmly fixed,
We do not drift at all!

We know the earth shall not be moved!
'Tis written in His Word!
This world is kept by mighty hands.
His mercy hath He poured!

And so, we spin, a mighty top!
This great blue ball, no man can stop!
Our saving place is fixed in space.
For Love preserves this human race!

*"Say among the heathen that the Lord reigneth: the world also shall be established that it shall not be moved."*
*Psalm 96:10*

# A Nature of Kindness

Our God!
His very nature is of kindness!
To creatures of His hand,
Comprised of dust!

The author, He,
Of galaxies unnumbered;
And yet,
His heart finds time
For such as us!

A fallen race,
Unworthy of His pity:
Drowning in our sins
And quite alone!

His nature could not bear
Our hopeless sorrow!
Nor could His Son's,
And so, He sent His Own!

All that They ask,
Is that our souls will listen!
Have faith in blood,
That truly has atoned!

To save us from the misery
Of our making!
And bring us, as dear children,
To His home!

*"Come now, and let us reason together, saith the Lord: Though your sins be as scarlet, they shall be as white as snow; Though they be red like crimson. They shall be as wool."*
*Isaiah 1:18*

# Little More than Forty

Today He comes to Jordan,
Baptized for all our sins.
The consecrated Son of God,
His ministry begins!

Tempted in the wilderness,
By the wicked prince of woe!
He enters now into His work:
Salvation for our souls!

Opening the Scriptures,
Enlightening our minds!
In little more than forty months,
A work for all of time!

In words of wondrous power,
He reaches to the heart!
Disciples call to carry truth
And have their sacred part!

Healing bodies! Healing souls!
Redemption comes, that all may know;
A Lord whose love is true and deep,
For all of us His fallen sheep!

Now He, who raised the sleeping dead,
Will die our second death instead!
Crucified by mindless hate;
Surely now, the hour's late!

In time of end, He'll come again:
Our loving Lord, our precious friend!

*"He which testifieth these things saith, Surely I come quickly. Amen. Even so, come, Lord Jesus."*
*Revelation 22:20*

\*\*\*

(The line "Little more than forty months" refers to the forty-two months or three-and-a-half years of Jesus' earthly ministry.)

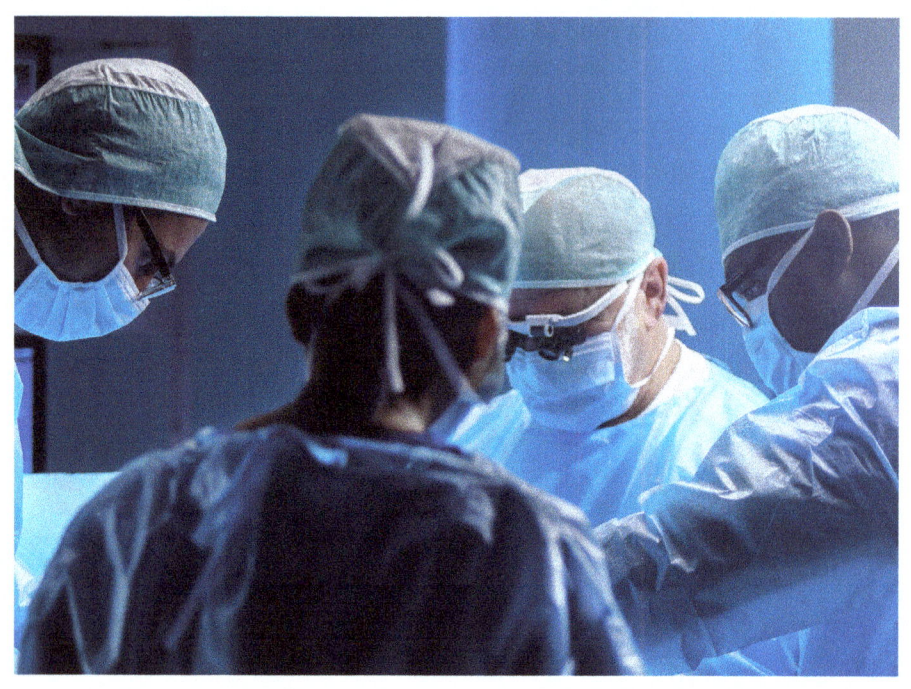

# The Surgeons and the Book

Some take a scalpel to it,
As though the Word were dead!
And not the sacred voice of God—
Just something old instead!

Oh, never do they hear it speak!
The gospel's hope, they do not seek!
But just old words and history,
And ancient forms of speech.

Some trivia, perhaps to glean,
Like shells found on a beach.
So, all the truth Love put within,
Is far beyond their reach!

Its glories hidden well from them;
So earnest in their search!
Perhaps, they should lay scalpels down
And find a Bible church!

*"For the word of God is quick, and powerful, and sharper than any twoedged sword, ...and is a discerner of the thoughts and intents of the heart."*
*Hebrews 4:12*

# Heart Cry

Good mothers all yearn for the fruit of their womb:
Good fathers with cries from the heart!
Their prayers rise to heaven, borne up by the blood.
"Oh, keep them while we are apart!"

No parent cries out from their soul to the skies,
With affection more deep and sincere,
Than the dear heart of Jesus, who pleads for the soul,
With blood and Divinity's tear.

"O Father! These children! Their lives art Thine own!
For this My own blood it did flow!
With power from on high, bring them here to the sky!
Give them faith in a heavenly home!"

"Behold Ye my wounds! Myself I lay down!
To save of these sheep for Thy throne!
Bring them out! Bring them up!
In the arms of Thy love.
Oh, let them not perish alone!"

"Oh, Father on high, accept of my cry!
I plead and with blood I atone!
Give faith like a fire to all who desire!
Abba! Bring all of our offspring back home!"

One pleads for your soul! His own He doth know.
His Father hath set Him just so!
Now pleading is He, for the soul to set free.
Yea! Our Jesus is pleading for thee!

*"For there is one God, and one mediator between God and men, the man Christ Jesus, who gave himself a ransom for all."*
*1 Timothy 2:5*

# Where Is Thy Trust?

'Tis well to work the works of God
And have your joy prolonged;
But we are not to trust in works,
Nor that our faith is strong!

True trust, is trust in Him alone
And not our strength in prayer;
But rather know, what ere befall,
His hand is always there!

A tike gives trust completely,
To you who hold their hand:
And that is just the very trust,
That God would have from man.

So come, and plead you boldly,
Before the throne of thrones;
But know what ere His answer be,
That He is God alone.

*"Our God whom we serve is able to deliver us, …But if not…"*
*Daniel 3:17–18*

# A Time for Peace

Death is not a time for doubt,
Rather, time for peace.
Time to wait the God of all,
Whose wonders never cease.

Time to rest your hand in His,
While waiting for the light,
Firm to trust within your heart,
the ending of the night.

It must be so! He would not lie!
Our risen Lord, gone to the sky.
And yet, so very close to us
As now our latest breath!

There is no faith that waits alone,
To meet the time of death!

*"I am not ashamed; for I know whom I have believed, and am persuaded that he is able to keep that which I have committed unto him against that day."*
*2 Timothy 1:12*

# Consuming Fire

How could a deity of love,
Burn us in endless fire?
How could eternal torture meet,
The justice He desires?

He knows we're frail and very small.
And would not do this thing at all!
To slander thus our Deity,
Is but to make Him one as we!

With heart of stone:
For beings to dread!
And one in whom,
All love were dead!

There is a Being of fire.
There is a torment true!
He is a sin consuming fire,
To burn your dross or you!

To wake when judgment calls you,
And know His love was true!
And that you have despised your Lord,
This were true hell for you!

There is no other torment,
Could burn as this could do!
Then just to look upon pure love,
That mourns the likes of you!

And those who choose to spurn that love,
Long offered them for free,
Will see the justice of His flame,
Consuming sin and thee!

And as the enemy of all:
Who lives in hate of we,
Will ashes be beneath men's feet,
So shalt thine own fate be!

*"Therefore will I bring forth a fire from the midst of thee, it shall devour thee, and I will bring thee to ashes upon the earth."*
*Ezekiel 28:18*

*"Ye shall tread down the wicked; for they be ashes under the soles of your feet in the day that I shall do this, saith the Lord of hosts."*
*Malachi 4:3*

# We Want a King

Canons roar their thunder,
And subjects line the streets!
A monarch leaves his royal coach,
A carpet 'neath his feet!

The crowds adore mere mortal flesh,
That's here today, then dies!
And offer homage, best reserved
For He who reigns on high!

The pomp and show of human kings,
Yet mortal flesh as we,
Are naught to Him who made this world
And speaks just what shall be!

The people seek a haughty king
And sin as they of old,
"Our God on high is not enough,
Mere man would we behold!"

But God has given us true Man,
Forever more to be:
His own dear Son, incarnate flesh,
And yet, true Deity!

Though some demand an earthly king,
To rule their world that be;
Our God has given Jesus Christ!
We need no king but He!

*"Never the less the people refused to obey the voice of Samuel; and they said, Nay, but we will have a king over us; that we also may be like all the nations."*
*1 Samuel 8:19–20*

# Good Master

Christ watched so many walk away,
To follow Him no more that day.
They turned from Him, away from life,
And wandered blindly to the night.

"And will you also go away?"
He asked the twelve. What would they say?
A Solemn sadness in His voice,
He asked that they should make their choice.

Now, Peter felt the urgent love,
That lived within that question,
And answered for them all that day,
Without a hesitation.

"Lord, wither would you have us go?
You speak the words that feed our souls!
No other Lord there is that be.
Good Master we will follow Thee!"

Today there's still no place to go,
If you would feed your famished soul,
But to the feet of He who speaks,
The words of life for all who seek.

And as our world turns from faith,
And this dark time grows very late—
That self-same voice to us doth say,
"And will you also go away?"

Oh! With one voice, let all reply,
Good Master there is only Thy
Sweet voice to feed our needful souls.
There is no other Lord we know!

The heathen search this world o're,
But we Thine own, we seek no more!
And look no other place to be—
Good Master we will follow Thee!

*"Then said Jesus unto the twelve, 'Will you also go away?'*
*Then Simon Peter answered him, 'Lord to whom shall we go?*
*Thou hast the words of eternal life.'"*
*John 6:67–68*

# The God Our Hearts Embrace

We get the God our hearts embrace;
All things are by belief!
If we would serve a cold, hard god,
Our lives, we'll live in grief!

And if we'd have no god at all,
Nor know of heaven's King,
The very angels, they would weep,
Our lives a hollow thing!

But if we'd know a Father-kind,
Who blesses through His Son,
And trust in He, as Mercy's heart,
The God we knew when young:

All heaven stands before us
For gates are opened wide!
And depths of love will come to us,
That evermore surprise!


"Lord, I knew thee that thou art a hard man."
Matthew 25:24

"And the serpent said unto the woman, Ye shall not surely die:
For God doth know that in the day ye eat thereof your eyes shall be opened,
and ye shall be as gods."
Genesis 3:4–5

"Yea I have loved thee with an everlasting love: therefore with
lovingkindness have I drawn thee."
Jeremiah 31:3

# Fugitives from Glory

One page of holy writ, sent to Philemon,
Appealing to the mercy of his heart.
"Receive him as myself, and if he owes you,
Do lay it unto me who takes his part!"

As tender a page as Paul has left us.
"Forgive, and I will bear what debt there be."
The spirit that moved that great disciple,
Was as my Master's own who pleads for me!

"This poor debtor has, but naught that he can offer.
Do lay his charge unto the blood of Me!
Receive him as My heart, in your forgiveness;
That he may be restored back unto Thee."

Now, all of us are fugitives from glory,
Who come to God through Christ—His worthy One!
And He on high receives in His Beloved,
All trusting flesh, as daughters and as sons!

*"That you might receive him forever."*
*Philemon 1:15, NKJV*

# Our Unbelieving Prayers

Peter's chained in prison.
The church knows this means doom!
And yet, they pray a miracle,
Assembled in their room!

An angel enters prison,
Where guards so strangely sleep!
Peter's woke and chains fall off,
Like wool sheared off from sheep!

Now, Peter's knocking at their gate,
While church is deep in prayer;
But won't believe God's heard their cry,
Although good Peter's there!

Martha said, "What God you ask…"
Yet, at her brother's tomb,
She pleads, "Do not remove the rock!
There's stench within that room!"

Why do we ask for miracles,
In which we don't believe?
Why do we ask without a hope?
And all the angels grieve?

Behold! The goodness of our God!
Who answers faithless prayer!
And pities hearts so easily,
But given to despair!

We ask for Heaven's manna,
Then just expect a stone!
And yet, the goodness of His heart,
Does not leave us alone!

Dear Lord, rebuke our unbelief,
For now, the hour's late!
Do teach our foolish doubting hearts,
To trust our God in faith!

*"Peter continued knocking: and when they had opened the door and saw him, they were astonished."*
*Acts 12:16*

# Graven Hands—Wounded Hands

Those graven hands, those wounded hands,
Whereon our names are writ:
They still reach out to fallen man;
They haven't changed a bit!

I know the Man with wounded hands,
Can heal a riven heart.
And if you'll take His hands in faith,
He'll do more than His part!

He's healed gravely damaged lives.
He'll lift your helpless soul:
And He can save from any sin;
Do more than you can know!

Those graven hands, those wounded hands,
Oft lifted me from harm.
And when in need, those loving hands,
Have held me in their arms!

He's more than all your circumstance:
Far more than mortal man!
And you can trust your life and soul,
To Him with wounded hands!

*"Behold, I have graven thee upon the palms of my hands."*
*Isaiah 49:16*

# He Sees It All

He sees the years awaiting us,
And charts the days of man.
Existing He, outside of time,
The future He can scan!

The end declared before the start,
To tell us what shall be.
This is the same who sent His Son,
To live and die for we!

Our God, He councils, guides, and leads,
All souls who will be led:
Who follow on, despite this world,
To choose His paths instead!

This Lord who knows that we are small,
As children He would lead.
If we would but renounce our pride,
And to His voice pay heed!

*"I am God, and there is none like me,
declaring the end from the beginning."
Isaiah 46:9–10*

# In His Heart

In the heart of Jesus!
In death, that's where we'll be!
Just as our lives were lived in Him,
And He did live in we!

I'll safely sleep within His breast,
Till He desires me!
Work of His hands, since time began,
His own do sleep in He!

The body here, of course, decays,
But His shall safely lie,
Asleep in Christ, till trump shall sound,
On earth from out the sky!

From the heart of Jesus,
His own shall come again!
For we are His dear children,
And He our dearest Friend!

Now I am full persuaded,
That He will safely keep,
The essence of His own within,
While we shall deeply sleep!

Until He says, "Children arise!
And bless the morning skies!
For you who placed your trust in Me,
Have never really died!"

"You only slept within my heart,
Where none could ere molest.
For you, I have reserved a home
Among the true and blessed!"

*"Whosoever liveth and believeth in me shall never die."*
*John 11:26*

*"And when Jesus had cried with a loud voice, he said, Father, into thy hands I commend my spirit:"*
*Luke 23:46*

*"I… am persuaded that he is able to keep that which I have committed to him against that day."*
*2 Timothy 1:12*

*"The spirit shall return unto God who gave it."*
*Ecclesiastes 12:7*

# Son of David

The blind man cried, "Thou Son of David,
Thy mercy have on me!"
That helpless cry comes down the years,
And strikes a chord in we!

They tried to stay his desperate cry,
And ordered he be still!
And yet he cried out all the more,
His need would not be stilled!

And ever to such helpless need,
Our true physician paid His heed!
He made the blind of eye to see,
And more than this He'll do for we!

There is a cry from needful hearts:
A cry no man can quench!
Conviction comes, of terrible sins
And their attended stench!

No one can make their own heart clean,
Nor save themselves from sin!
And with that understanding comes,
A desperate cry within!

No longer are we of the blind,
Now clearly, we can see our crime!
Now, as that blind man, crieth we
Unto the only help there be!

Oh, Savior see our helpless need
And to our souls, physician heed!
Thou Son of David crieth we,
"Have mercy Thou on even me!"


*"He cried, saying, Jesus, thou Son of David, have mercy on me."*
*Luke 18:38*

# Some Treasures Can't Be Lost

There's treasure that can not be lost
Although the heavens fall!

There's love that lives in memory,
When dark is over all.

There's smiles not forgotten,
The gentle touch of hand:

The everlasting love of Christ,
Who suffered so for man.

The lives on earth we bind to
Will never be forgot,

Though pain and grief, within this world
May be the human lot.

Yet, joy that can't be measured,
Awaits the faithful heart,

When every precious soul in Christ,
Shall rise to never part!

*"And God shall wipe away all tears from their eyes; And there shall be no more death, neither sorrow, nor crying, Neither shall there be any more pain: for the former things are passed away."*
*Revelation 21:4*

# Wrong Side of the Door!

Back in the day, when I was young,
Knew not what breath was for.
'Twas then I should have heard His knock,
On the outside of my door!

One night temptation overwhelmed,
Near choked my will from me!
And barely had I voice to call,
"Oh, God bring help to me!"

Although my words were but a gasp,
Such tightness in my throat!
The good Lord cast temptation out!
The second that I spoke!

Can't say I beat the devil!
I know but One who did!
And if He had not love for me,
I would not want to live!

Foul evil never seems to knock!
But Love does ever more!
Don't let the Master stand without,
On the wrong side of the door!


*"Behold, I stand at the door, and knock: if any man hear my voice, and open the door, I will come in to him, and will sup with him, and he with me."*
*Revelation 3:20*

# Thy Flag Unfurled

Our hearts belong to Thee, O King.
We see Thy flag unfurled!
And splendidly, in gold we read:
"The Savior of the World!"

We hear Thine anthem sung on high;
There, writ by angel hand!
"Receive O Earth, God's gift to thee;
The hope and stay of Man!"

Cruel spikes and thorns and evil's scorn,
Upon the truth, these, rain!
Yet, evermore God doth declare,
"They rage, but all in vain!"

Thy love it rises o're the earth,
To draw upon all men!
Oh! Blessed all, who come to Thee,
Our Brother and our Friend!


*"Thou hast given a banner to them that fear thee, that it may
be displayed because of the truth. Selah."*
*Psalm 60:4*

# Yahweh Had a Son

Yahweh had a Son, ere there was Mary.
Yahweh had a child of His own!
And in the courts of glory, in song they tell the story;
How Yahweh gave His Son and dwelt alone!

Yahshua was a Spirit, born of Spirit.
The very stuff of Yahweh was his own!
And He could pay the price, for every human vice,
But only as a man could He atone!

The angel said, "His name will be Yahshua,"
"Salvation of Yahweh" for His own!
The Son became a man, according to that plan:
Cut from the Mountain came our mighty Stone!

Yahshua said, "A body thou hast fashioned.
To do thy will, I come as it is writ:
To save this race, and praise the name of Yahweh:
And turn all men to Thee as it is fit!"

"I do not seek my will, but thine's who sent me.
I come to speak to them Thy holy name!
The Ancient of Days declare I to them:
My Father and their Elohim, the same!"

*"Who hath established all the ends of the earth? What is his name,
and what is his son's name, if thou canst tell?"*
*Proverbs 30:4*

# The Anguished Cry

"Depart from me good Master!
I am a sinful man!"
So saith Peter to the Lord:
In guilt he could not stand!

He says, "Depart good Master!"
Yet, fears, lest, at his word,
The Light of Lights depart from him,
And sever Heaven's cord.

"Depart from me good Master!"
So oft my heart hath cried.
And if He took me at my word,
All hope indeed had died!

He does not heed that anguished cry,
Of such as you or fools like I.
Remembering He, that we are dust,
His soul is moved; His heart is touched!

He knows its guilt that's talking–
Heeds not our hasty words.
Instead, reads deeply of our hearts.
Oh! Praise we so the Lord!

"I will not now forsake thee,
Nor leave thee yet to pine.
For there is mercy with thy Lord;
And I have called thee mine!"

*"Simon Peter… fell down at Jesus knees, saying, Depart from me,
for I am a sinful man, O Lord."*
*Luke 5:8*

# The Offer

In France, some terrorists held helpless captives!
An officer went in to "talk" them free.

And there a woman wailed aloud in terror!
He said, "Just let her go; instead, take me."

And that agreed; he died to save that woman.
By sacrifice of self, he let her live.

And all of France declared this fine man noble,
Because to save her life, himself he'd give!

Once, within a garden named for olives,
Another said, "Take Me and let them go."

Two thousand years our world has praised a Savior,
Who gave Himself to save each trembling soul!

Now, ever in this world of sin and sorrow,
We hear that plea spoke out for such as we!

"Oh, let them go! Myself I freely offer!
Oh, let them live! and wraith descend on Me!"

*"Jesus answered, I have told you that I am he: if therefore ye seek me, let these go their way."*
*John 18:8*

# A Dream in Galilee

A man with questions fell asleep and dreamed of Galilee.
And found the Master standing yet, beside a peaceful sea.
His hair was stirred by a gentle breeze; he was robe and sandal clad:
And the look beheld within those eyes, none other ever had.

The dreamer stared; his senses stunned! Could this be whom He seemed?
"It's really You?" he dared to ask, "Or is this but a dream?"
"I come to those who search for Me." The timeless Teacher said.
"In Bible, prayer, in many ways. you slumber now in bed."

"Lord," he asked, "You watch us still, now twenty centuries hence?"
The smile was sad, and deep within, he mourned his lack of sense.
"Some say God's dead, and now they hold the means to swiftly end,
The lives of all who dwell on Earth, whenever they intend!"

Can hope be held? Can men still learn, to call their brother friend?
Or will the lost, who worship hate, destroy the race of men?"
His Master's words transcended fear; a flame that would not quail,
And taught the man who questioned him, that faith can never fail.

Make no mistake, for what men sow, still surely shall they reap.
My Father lives! We know our own and seek for all our sheep.
None are lost, who live in faith. Have trust in me and see.
Then wrapped in hope, the sleeper smiled, a dream in Galilee.

*"I am he that liveth, and was dead; and behold, I am alive forever more."*
*Revelation 1:18*

(The author's first poem. Written April 1, 1971)

# Waking to the Light

Today there is a funeral,
Within the city Nain,
A young man going to the grave,
His mother deep in pain.

A widow she, her only son,
Now destined for the ground.
A grim parade of mourning winds,
unto the gates of town.

And coming also to the gate,
From just the other way,
The Nazarene of miracles,
And friends all on their way!

The boy lies on an open bier,
His mother blind with tears,
The future holding now for her
But loneliness and fear.

This grieving helpless woman,
Much moves the Master's heart.
And just as though she were His own,
He takes this mother's part.

"Come, do not weep," He says to her,
And halts the mourners grim.
His hand upon the dead boy's bier,
The Lord speaks unto him.

In tones of pure authority,
As clear as morning skies,
He says to that cold, silent corpse,
"Young man I say arise!"

Glad miracle! The boy sits up!
Now waking to the light!
And Christ presents him to the one
Who lost him to the night!

And all who see, or hear of this,
Can know Messiah true!
Both, they who witnessed long ago,
And readers, such as you!

*"And there came a fear on all: and they glorified God,
saying that a great prophet is risen up among us."
Luke 7:16*

# A Righteousness Received

The earth cannot call down the rain,
This cannot be our trust.
Nor can it hope to bring forth grain,
For it is only dust.

As Heaven sends it life in rain,
To make a garden on it's plain;
The righteousness of our desire,
Must be the gift of God entire!

That is the righteousness of Christ;
Which comes from Heaven free!
It is the gracious gift of God,
Bestowed on you and me!

A million years of noble deeds,
Could never purge the soul!
The new heart is a gift divine.
His grace that we may know:

There is no boast allowed of men;
But glory in one gracious friend!
"Let him that boast, let his boast be,
That, in his heart he knoweth Me!"

*"Let him that boasts, boast in this, that he understands and knows me."*
*Jeremiah 9:24, NKJV*

# The Living Stone

The Stone cut from the Mountain,
Without a single hand,
Was He who often called Himself,
On earth, "the Son of Man."

"The Living Stone," said Peter,
"Disallowed of men."
Yet, chosen by the One on High,
And "precious" now as then!

A "stumbling stone, Rock of Offence,"
For those who spurn the Word!
But Mighty One, our Elohim,
To we who call Him Lord!

The Corner Stone of endless life,
The Savior, He of man!
Foundation of the human race,
The Son of great I Am!

Yahweh, the founding Mountain,
Yahshua, He the Stone!
Deliverer of those who trust,
In just His blood alone!

*"The stone was cut out of the mountain without hands."*
*Daniel 2:45*

*"A living stone, disallowed indeed of men,*
*but chosen of God, and precious."*
*1 Peter 2:4*

# A Sacrifice That Breaks the Heart

Now would you sacrifice for God?
Not merely cash or coin,
But rather, offer up your child,
The dear one of your loins?

As once did faithful Abraham?
Or loving mother Hanna?
Who gave her precious firstborn son,
Her gift of heaven's manna!

She made a little robe for him,
And brought it to him yearly.
And gave him back to serve the Lord,
Although she missed him dearly!

Such sacrifice, of broken hearts,
Reflect that of our Father!
Who likewise offered up His own!
A gift for ever after!

A broken and a contrite heart,
That truly sees the cross,
Has come to sense Almighty's pain,
And taste of heaven's loss!

God gave back Abraham, his son.
And Hanna, sons and daughters.
But He has poured His love to us,
As endless living waters!

Small wonder then, that broken hearts,
All such that God has known,
He does accept, and take to Him,
As though it were his own!

*"A broken and a contrite heart, O God, thou wilt not despise."*
*Psalm 51:17*

# The God of Slaves

The Pharaoh of Egypt scorned the God of the slaves;
Said Moses and Aaron were mad men who raved!
Till the god-king of Egypt, was swept from his throne,
By He of the Hebrews: the true God alone!

Philistine oppressors, thought "God in a box"
Would bow to their "Dagon" in a temple they locked!
Their idol they found, shorn of head, hands, and feet,
For the great God of slaves, never bows in defeat!

The slaves of our nation, though used and oppressed,
Yet, learned of the God, who hears our distress.
The enemy of chains, and of slave masters He!
So, the bound of our nation, from bondage He freed!

Are you now a slave to drugs or to drink?
Chained by your vices, and helpless you think?
He still hears the cries of the bound and oppressed!
And the God of the Hebrews, still knows how to bless!

Our God can deliver by the strength of His hand,
The hearts and the flesh, of each woman and man!
Who call in their bondage: He hears when they pray!
And He will deliver! The dear God of slaves!


*"Call upon me in the day of trouble: I will deliver thee,
and thou shall glorify me."*
*Psalm 50:15*

# A Very Special Man

Mary found to her surprise,
A very special man,
Who only sought her pain and need,
And hid no secret plan.

He knew that she was soaked in sin,
And used to being used.
And yet, His very glance spoke out,
To her of great good news!

He offered her a pure new heart
And drew her soul from out the dark.
His difference from other men
Was startling and stark!

No look of lust or quick disgust,
Her soul gave thankful sigh,
And weary head fell on His breast.
She could not help but cry!

She'd thought herself past caring.
She'd thought herself past tears.
And yet she'd longed for purity,
Throughout those terrible years!

And as she wept, and could not stop,
As from a darkened den,
She felt her demons turn and flee,
From Him, her newfound Friend!

At length she fell, exhausted.
But when she woke from sleep,
She found, He yet, sat close beside,
A faithful watch to keep.

Her smile was a newborn smile,
which He returned in kind.
Her gratitude and love for Him,
To last the years of time.


*"Mary Magdalene, out of whom he cast seven devils."*
*Mark 16:9*

# The Sinner at Simon's House

A sinner dwells at Simon's house, unknown unto men—
A stiffened neck, a hardened heart, a back that will not bend!
Though saved from his own rotting flesh, a leper's living death,
He will not fall upon the Rock and let his heart be cleft.

Although he sees unbridled love in Mary's every gesture,
His frozen heart does not respond. The pharisee condemns her.
She wipes her tears from blessed feet, with long and flowing hair,
And kisses them, as though there's not, another person there.

He's cleansed the darkness from her soul. Those days no longer matter.
And Christ receives her grateful love, poured out from alabaster.
To Simon, Christ declares, "Her sins, as many as they be,
Are cancelled now, by loving much, her soul has been set free."

"But, he who loveth little, will find his sins remain,
And though his flesh be newly cleansed, his mind is still the same."
The soft rebuke of Jesus's words, goes right to Simon's heart.
Revealed leprosy within, near tears his soul apart!

And now, that once proud judge of sins, would fain bring ointment too;
And do the very loving work that he saw Mary do!
Her Lord declares, that Mary's part, will stand the test of time
And go where e're the gospel goes, to every land and clime!

She's overcome fear of rebuke and let devotion show;
And love of Christ that burns within, has saved her very soul!

*"Wherefore I say unto thee, her sins, which are many, are forgiven:*
*for she loved much."*
*Luke 7:47*

# The World Before

There was an earth, before this earth,
Where vice had multiplied:
Where hearts were dead to human need
And kindness cast aside!

A larger, stronger, human race,
In love with self and sin,
All-trace of love, long given up,
For even natural kin!

Long lived, in great vitality,
With centuries for their span;
The devil laughed, and heaven wept,
For fallen earth and man!

No cry of women heeded,
No needs of children filled,
No value held for human life,
Or endless blood they spilled!

It grieved our Father in His heart,
Who then decreed an end;
Except for Noah and his own,
Who found both grace and Friend!

And now our race declines again,
Flesh boasting in its pride!
Both Christ and cross and holy truth,
Forgotten or despised!

Preserve O Lord Your children,
Who love and trust thy name!
When falls from heaven, once again,
Not water, but the flame!

*"For behold, the day cometh, that shall burn as an oven."*
*Malachi 4:1*

# The Child Grows

The Child grows, and must be kept from fire.
The very same, who lit the flaming stars!
Including that which lights the sky above us,
And warms the very earth, just where we are!

Yea! He who spoke water into existence,
And made the great wide oceans, that astound!
Must carefully be watched, while He is bathing,
Within a shallow pool, lest He should drown!

Necessities of body must be tended,
And fed, the one who made all crops to grow!
His power of creation hid in heaven,
From He, who now, is such a little soul!

And now behold, the Son of Glory arising,
From ground, He slowly, struggles up to stand!
And takes the first of steps 'twill lead to Calvary,
When He is grown up, the Son of Man!

And every baby step is seen in heaven,
As He struggles, to learn and understand!
With Mary and Joseph, close beside Him,
He'll slowly, come to see His Father's plan!

Now, learns He, names of things, that He created;
And at His mother's knee forms little prayers!
All this! While angels watching Him intently,
Can barely turn away their holy stare!

Teased, and yet adored by older siblings,
Each dawn He comes to learn of bright new things!
While yet, in shining realms beyond His knowing,
He does not hear delight that angels sing!

*"And Jesus increased in wisdom and stature,
and in favor with God and man."
Luke 2:52*

# Facing the Tempter

When Christ was weakened, from forty days of fasting,
    The vile tempter saw at last, his chance!
Appearing as from the very light of heaven,
    In bright disguise he struck a holy stance!

"Thy Father calls an end now, to Thy fasting!
    And says, Thou may eat freely for Thy need.
Now IF Thou truly be the Son of Heaven
Go now! And turn these rocks to bread and feed!"

But Christ perceived at once, 'tis was the tempter!
    And knew that "IF" was bitterness of soul.
"Man does not live by bread alone," 'tis written,
    "But every word of God, as you must know!"

Then on the highest pinnacle of temple,
He tempts the Lord to cast His body down!
"For it is written, That He shall keep Thee safely.
And wilt not let Thy foot dash to the ground!"

But from that pinnacle, above the temple,
Our Lord gave answer with a weary sigh.
"And thou wilt find, 'tis also clearly written,
Thou shalt not tempt thy God with foolish pride!"

They stand at last upon a lofty mountain,
Kingdoms seen, which the devil claims his own.
"All this I give, if You will fall and worship.
For this the earth, I claim my sovereign throne!"

"Oh, get thee from My presence worthless tempter!
'Tis written thou shalt worship God alone!"
And at this blunt command the tempter raging,
Knows that he must obey that mighty tone!

For these words, spoke out in holy power,
Carried the full authority of Christ!
And when you are dismissed by He, the Master,
You do not think to have Him tell you twice!

Then angels from the throne of Jesus' Father,
Ministered unto His weakened state;
Who answered always "Yea!" and "It is written."
When darkness and the devil He'd abate!

*"Thou shalt not tempt the Lord thy God."*
*Matthew 4:7*

# Wine and Wisdom

Miriam, mother of our Lord,
Knew her Yahshua well!
She knew He was a precious Son,
More than her lips could tell!
She knew His love was great and deep,
Hence, brought to Him request.
And knew what e're her Son would do,
Would meet loves every test!

But at this joyous wedding,
He seemed to turn away,
And told her that this time and place,
Were not His chosen day.
Weddings then, went on for days,
And drink had just run out.
Their frantic host, although he searched,
Could find no more about.

'Twas then Christ's loving mother came
Unto her Son in trust.
And knew He would not turn away,
And leave the wedding thus.
That's why she spoke to servants:
Pure faith, in Him come through.
And said, "What e're my Son commands,
See that's the thing you do!"

We know Christ made pure water, wine!
A vintage better than the vine!
A tender act of kindness,
To please His mother's heart.
And save the wedding of their friends.
His love had done its part!

And then there were His mother's words:
Good words for me and you!
We know the world is darker now,
Yet, still, those words ring true!
The best advice you'll ever find,
And words you'll never rue.
"What e're my Son says to your heart,
See Christian that you do!"


*"His mother saith unto the servants, Whatsoever he saith unto you, do it."*
*John 2:5*

# Lazarus Come Forth!

Their message sent, two women wait, as life draws slow away.
If only their dear Carpenter, were here to help today!
Their brother now, can barely breathe, and it tears their spirits sore,
To watch their own dear Lazarus fade, perhaps to breathe no more!

But surely, Christ will quickly come, to save His ailing friend!
Then He will lift their brother up, to health restored again.
But Lazarus, at last has died! No miracle has come.
Its' been four days of misery now, since breath was finally done.

And now the Man of miracles, at last is come again,
And sees these two dear women weep, for Lazarus, His friend.
"If only you were here O Lord, our loved one had not died."
And as they gathered at the tomb, then even Jesus cried!

He's told those grieving sisters, "All unbelief do leave.
Thy very kin shall rise again, if this you do believe.
I am the resurrection; I am the life of man.
Thy kin shall breathe and walk again. 'Tis all as Heaven planned!"

The sealing stone is rolled away, there's silence in the den.
And Jesus gives His Father thanks and then calls forth His friend!
All hear some movement in that room.
Then comes the risen from the tomb!

Before the very den of death, all gasp in mortal fear.
A man, still fully wrapped for grave, emerges, standing near!
Unbound, he now from funeral wrap, wide-eyed, all clearly see;
It is no hoax, nor yet a ghost, but Lazarus it be!!

Before their eyes, blessed miracle! A joy above all other:
For Mary and her sister have, restored to them, their brother!
That family of Lazarus is now comprised of four!
For Jesus in this house is kin! And shall be ever more!

*"Jesus said to her, 'Did I not say to you that if you would believe
You would see the glory of God?'"
John 11:40, NKJV*

# The Olive Grove

First there was Gethsemane,
And then there was the cross!
But it was in the olive grove,
Where Satan's hope was lost!

"Oh! Let this cup pass from Me!
It's drags I would not drain!
I would not have Thy wrath on me!
Yet, I'll accept their blame."

"Thy sovereign will, and not My own!
Oh! Father let it be!
And let the cross of all men's guilt,
Be fully laid on me!"

"I came to do Thy will O God:
And this Thy will I'll do!
But Oh! Remember, Thou My soul!
I trust it unto You!"

Now come our crimes, our horrible deeds:
Now He becomes our sin!
Love's terrible trade, as we are made,
God's righteousness in Him!

The weight comes down by slow degree.
He nearly dies from shame!
Had not an angel come to Him,
To strengthen Him for pain!

His dear ones slept, as blood and sweat,
Came forth upon His brow.
And this He suffered all for we!
And no man knows just how!

But all the guilt 'twill ever be,
For all our world's sin,
Came down like rock to crush His soul
And take the breath of Him!

That olive grove of agony,
That night of deep despair—
Became the hope of all mankind,
Because He chose to care!

*"O my Father, if this cup may not pass away from me, except I drink it, thy will be done."*
Matthew 26:42

# Upon This Hill for Dying

Upon this hill for dying,
Three men this day condemned!
Two common thieves; but He the third,
Our most uncommon Friend!

The sound of hammers pounding,
And two loud shrieking men,
And One who bears in silent pain,
The weight of all that's been!

The press and guilt of all mankind,
Upon His heart bears He!
And Christ will die for every sin,
That there will ever be!

A cold, unnatural darkness,
In the burning heat of day:
As if the very sun itself,
In grief would turn away!

The innocence of purity,
now lifts my sins from me!
While angels look upon a scene,
Unfit for eyes to see!

He cries out for His Father now.
Upon His soul, pure dread!
One word of faith, one weary sigh,
And God's great gift is dead!

Oh, cry out, will you, with me now?
All flesh with voice as one!
"OH Father! Who hath sent Thy love:
OH God! What have we done?"

*"They shall look upon me whom they have pierced, and they shall mourn for him, as one mourneth for his only son."*
*Zechariah 12:10*

# The Rising of the Son

A blessed wounded body, within a borrowed tomb;
A massive rock across its face, to seal up the room.
In darkness watchful soldiers yawn, while vengeful demons frown.
At first, a tiny tremor comes: slight movement of the ground.

The darkest hour before the dawn, the earth begins to quake!
And weary guarding soldiers now, are firmly wide awake.
A messenger from heaven's gate, arrives in blinding light!
With screams of fear, the demon host, have fled into the night!

And soldiers now, quite stiff with fear, fall to the ground as dead.
For they behold that angel bright who towers o'er their heads!
Now facing sealed sepulcher, in voice to pierce the tomb,
The angel speaks unto the One, Who sleeps within that room.

"Oh, Son of God, awake within! Thy Father calleth Thee!
And for this blessed purpose now, to You He sendeth me!"
The mighty rock he's slid away, as though a burden small.
Then comes a stirring from within, at that angelic call!

No gloom of death! A greater light comes from that borrowed tomb!
The entrance now is lit as though the dawn stepped from that room!
Oh, let the pens of poets speak! And let our authors rave!
Our blessed One, God's only Son, has risen from the grave!

"The resurrection and the life, I Am!" proclaimeth He!
And nothing now upon the earth is as it used to be!
Mankind redeemed; Salvation come! A new day has begun!
And we, His own, in joy proclaim, the rising of the Son!

*"But unto you that fear my name shall the Sun of righteousness
arise With healing in his wings."*
*Malachi 4:2*

# Traveling to Emmaus

Their hearts were sad and heavy,
Their dear One crucified!
And as they walked in sorrow then,
Another joined their side.

He asked their cause for mourning.
They answered, "Don't you know?
They've nailed up our Christ and Lord!
And hearts are sunken low."

"Great prophet He in word and deed!
Our hope, He did renew;
That He was our Deliverer,
To free from Roman rule!"

The Stranger then, took both in hand,
Unlocking scriptural proof,
And showed to them these things ordained,
From holy words of truth.

The prophecies He called to mind,
That all should come to pass,
Until their hearts had clearly seen,
The plan of God at last!

'Tis True, He'd called them foolish men,
With hearts slow to believe.
And yet they asked, He stay and dine,
When He would take His leave!

And as He blessed and broke the bread,
Their eyes saw it was He!
Now I would ask of modern man,
Have you not eyes to see?

How can one breach your stubborn walls,
That faith may come to be?
What can be done to bring your hearts
In faith to Calvary?

You say, the sight of broken bread,
Means not a thing to me!
Come then! And stand before His cross
And see Him broke for thee!

*"Their eyes were opened and they knew Him;
and he vanished from their sight."
Luke 24:30–31, NKJV*

# The Thorn

Before good Paul, there once was Saul:
A hide-bound Pharisee!
Who thought to persecute Christ's church,
Until light came to be!

Upon the road, Saul lost his sight
In vision of the Lord;
By miracle of healing then,
His eyesight was restored!

But then, deep in his ministry,
Clear vision fades away.
Slowly and relentlessly,
He lost clear view of day.

"Three times I did beseech the Lord,"
Said testament of he.
"And this His mighty answer then,
My Lord declared to me!"

"You walked in prideful darkness, once:
A Pharisee of men.
And you were, yes! Most surely blind!
Until I did befriend."

"I am the light and sight of Man!
Walk closer yet, with Me.
My grace is all-sufficient, Paul.
And it sufficeth thee!"

Now, Paul could see more clearly,
Than when he had full sight!
And as his Lord drew closer still,
He'd gladly brave the night!

"Oh truly, now I glory in,
This thorn You grant to me!
Enough and more, my Mighty Lord,
That I may bide with Thee!"

*"And He said unto me, my grace is sufficient for thee: for my strength is made perfect in weakness."*
*2 Corinthians 12:9*

# Before the Throne of Nero

In chains they bring the aging Paul,
To stand before mad Caesar.
And here he'll scatter seeds of life,
And plant his Ebeneezer!

Though not a man stands with him,
As he comes to judgments throne,
Yet, holy angels close attend.
Paul's never walks alone.

The gathered wait his helpless plea.
Instead, he thinks of them!
And offers all, his mighty Lord,
His Christ, the sinner's Friend!

And some within that evil place,
Will ask the Savior in!
Yes! Even here! Dear faithful Paul,
Finds souls his Lord can win!

Now even Nero, quite depraved,
Is strangely moved with fear,
It seems to him that he can feel
His judgment drawing near.

Yea! Even his dark twisted mind
Can sense an unseen power.
He dares not judge this fearless Paul.
The lion cannot devour!

Oh, may we too, so care for souls,
When we are facing death,
That self's forgot in preaching Christ,
The Rock for all that's cleft!

*"The Lord stood with me, and strengthened me;
that by me, the preaching might be fully known,
And that all the gentiles might hear: and I was delivered
out of the mouth of the lion."
2 Timothy 4:17*

# The Trump Shall Sound

The trump shall sound, and shake the ground,
And wake the glad of heart! And call as well,
Those who remain, whom Love hath set apart!
They know His voice. He's lived within!
(For they are kindred unto Him!)
Who comes to Earth to reap His own.
And gather what His blood hath sown!

Great angels line the pathway, that leads up to the sky!
No more will any righteous soul be called in faith to die!
The Son of God descends the path that climbs celestial heights,
And calls His children out of dark, no more to dwell in night!
With Him they rise! And fill the skies, like sparks ascend from fire!
And look on Him, they've longed to see, with all their hearts desire!

While others cry out to the rocks, to hide them from His face.
For His He is the loving Rock, the head of all their race!
"The resurrection and the life!" (as He Himself has said!)
The hope of all in whom He lived, now calls His from the dead!
"Arise! Awake! Who sleep in dust, in whom my Spirit dwelt!
I come to gather all of you unto my very self!"


"Forever more to dwell with me, and I to dwell with you!
A thousand years as just a day! For I your life renew!
Come! Meet the One who gave it all, who gave Me unto thee!
My Father! And your own as well! For you are kin to Me!"

Ascending to a sea of glass, unto the light of day!
"Come ye the blessed of my Son, forever more to stay!
All things to dine, have been prepared! And there are robes for thee!
For you have loved my precious Son! And you are dear to Me!"


*"For the Lord himself shall descend from heaven with a shout,
with the voice of the archangel, and with the trump of God:
and the dead in Christ shall rise first: Then we which are alive
and remain shall be caught up together with them in the clouds,
to meet the Lord in the air; and so shall we ever be with the Lord."
1 Thessalonians 4:16–17*

## TEACH Services, Inc.
P U B L I S H I N G

We invite you to view the complete
selection of titles we publish at:
**www.TEACHServices.com**


We encourage you to write us
with your thoughts about this,
or any other book we publish at:
**info@TEACHServices.com**


TEACH Services' titles may be purchased in
bulk quantities for educational, fund-raising,
business, or promotional use.
**bulksales@TEACHServices.com**


Finally, if you are interested in seeing
your own book in print, please contact us at:
**publishing@TEACHServices.com**

We are happy to review your manuscript at no charge.

www.ingramcontent.com/pod-product-compliance
Lightning Source LLC
Chambersburg PA
CBHW071201160426
43196CB00011B/2147